高山 靖子
亀井 曉子
高瀬 奈美
服部 守悦
峯 郁郎
Edward Sarich
Gary McLeod
Jack Ryan
Mark Sheehan

DESIGN ENGLISH
クリエイターのための闘う英語

南雲堂

素材協力者

青木和義
伊藤達哉
稲垣葵
大嶋慎一郎
片平光紀
川口峻
佐々木明
佐藤毅秀
佐野公理
中井俊宏
堀田徹
松田優
宮田夏鈴
森田凌伍
山本瑞季
吉川由衣菜
建築研究会 kenken 有志

Photo:
- p.118 Shizuoka University of Art and Culture (Logo 1)
- p.121 Kenneth William Caleno / Shutterstock.com
- p.138 Leonard Zhukovsky / Shutterstock.com (Guggenheim Museum)
- p.139 meunierd / Shutterstock.com (Centre Georges Pompidou)
- p.139 HUANG Zheng / Shutterstock.com (The chapel of Notre Dame du Haut)
- p.147 Pres Panayotov / Shutterstock.com（敷地２）

はじめに

デザインを学んでいるみなさん、すでにデザインの現場にいるみなさん、デザインに国境はありませんよね。世界中の人々とデザインを考えるためには、英会話力も必要だと思いませんか？

本書は、静岡文化芸術大学デザイン学部の教員が、デザインの現場における経験をもとにデザイン検討をするときによく使う言葉を盛り込み、国際文化学科の英語担当教員が、教育経験をもとに会話に役立つポイントをわかりやすくまとめました。

本書一冊でデザイン検討のできるパーフェクトな英語が身につくわけではありません。しかし、表現したいことがたくさんあるみなさんなら、本書をきっかけに会話の糸口をつかみ、学習へのモチベーションを高めることができるでしょう。

これからデザインの仕事に関わるみなさんに、あるいはすでに活躍しているみなさんに、楽しく意欲を持って英語学習に取り組んでいただきたい。そして、世界中の人々とディスカッションしながらデザインを高めていただきたい。
これが、本書を作成した私たちの願いです。

静岡文化芸術大学

高山靖子

本書の使い方

本書では、Unit ごとにテーマを設定し、それに関連する表現を使った Sample Dialogue を掲載しました。これをもとに、会話に役立つポイントを Keywords、Useful Phrases、Speaking Points にわかりやすくまとめてありますので、最低限の習得目標とするとよいでしょう。

Activities は、各 Unit で学習したことを応用してディスカッションや説明を行うトレーニングです。本書の巻末には、Activities で使われる可能性の高い言葉や辞書では調べにくい表現を Activity Guide としてまとめてありますので、適宜活用してください。

Keywords, Useful Phrases, Speaking Points

まずはこれに目を通して、各 Unit の学習ポイントをチェック。

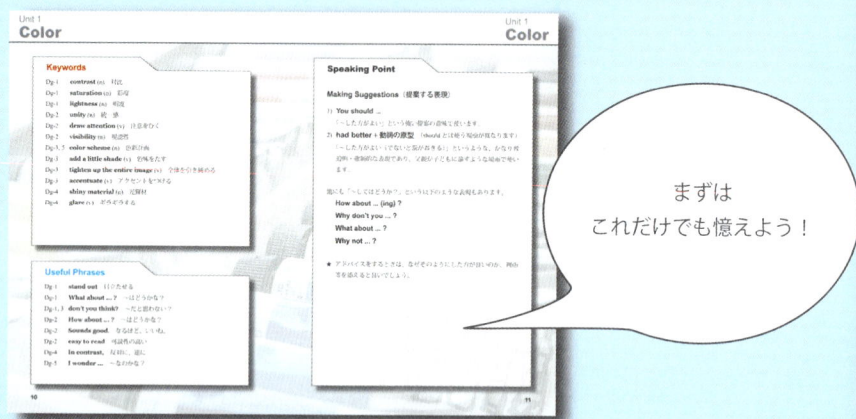

まずはこれだけでも憶えよう！

Sample Dialogue

ここで①の使い方や使われる状況を学習。
下段の質問に答えて、理解度をチェック。

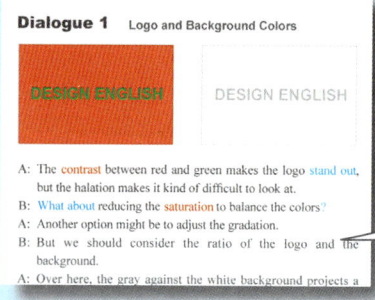

Sample Dialogue 内の Keywords は赤文字、Useful Phrases は青文字で書かれています。

③ Activities

各 Unit で学習した内容を Activities でどんどん使いましょう。

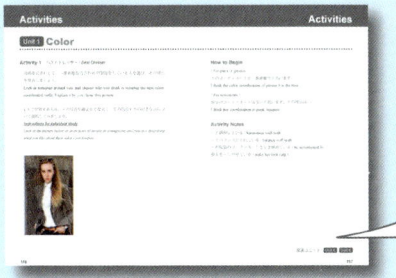

間違えても気にしない！
イラストやボディランゲージも交えて、サバイバル英語を身につけよう！

④ Activity Guide

巻末の Activity Guide に Activities で使う可能性の高い言葉が各 Unit のテーマごとにリスト化されていますので、適宜利用しましょう。

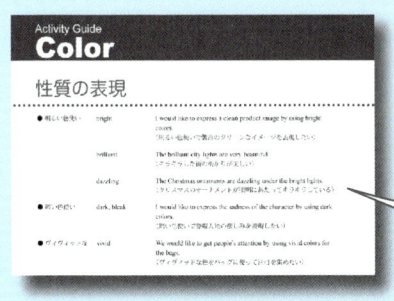

Unit テーマに直接関係する言葉だけでなく、一緒に使う頻度の高い言葉も掲載されています。

⑤ Column

ところどころにコラムとして、間違えやすい言葉や、日本語では同じ言葉でも英語ではその感覚によって使い分けられている言葉を掲載しました。憶えておくとより深いディスカッションができるようになりますので、学習の合間に読んでおくとよいでしょう。

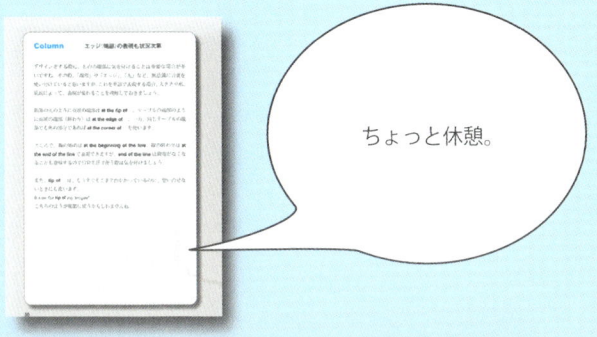

ちょっと休憩。

Table of Contents

はじめに 3
本書の使い方 4
Unit 1 **Color** 9
   Column: 彩度と発色 17
   Column: シンボルマークは和製英語？ 17
   Column: ハレーションは使わない？ 18
   Column: Character Colorは日本語？ 18
Unit 2 **Form** 19
   Column: エッジ（端部）の表現も状況次第 30
Unit 3 **Material** 31
Unit 4 **Operation** 41
   Column: いろいろな操作 50
Unit 5 **Composition** 51
   Column: どのくらい下の方にある？ 60
Unit 6 **Sense** 61
Unit 7 **Scale** 69
   Column: 何の大きさ？どんな大きさ？ 78
Unit 8 **Situation** 79
Unit 9 **Light and Shadow** 87
   Column: きらきら？ぎらぎら？ 96
Unit 10 **Function** 97
   Column: 仕様や特徴、性能を示すとき 104
Unit 11 **Application** 105

Activities 115
Activity Guide 157

Unit 1
Color

この章では、色について検討するための表現を学習します。

Unit 1
Color

Keywords

Dg-1	**contrast** (n)	対比
Dg-1	**saturation** (n)	彩度
Dg-1	**lightness** (n)	明度
Dg-2	**unity** (n)	統一感
Dg-2	**draw attention** (v)	注意をひく
Dg-2	**visibility** (n)	視認性
Dg-3, 5	**color scheme** (n)	色彩計画
Dg-3	**add a little shade** (v)	色味をたす
Dg-3	**tighten up the entire image** (v)	全体を引き締める
Dg-3	**accentuate** (v)	アクセントをつける
Dg-4	**shiny material** (n)	光輝材
Dg-4	**glare** (v)	ギラギラする

Useful Phrases

Dg-1	**stand out**	目立たせる
Dg-1	**What about … ?**	〜はどうかな？
Dg-1, 3	**don't you think?**	〜だと思わない？
Dg-2	**How about … ?**	〜はどうかな？
Dg-2	**Sounds good.**	なるほど。いいね。
Dg-2	**easy to read**	可読性の高い
Dg-4	**In contrast,**	反対に、逆に
Dg-5	**I wonder …**	〜なのかな？

Unit 1
Color

Speaking Point

Making Suggestions（提案する表現）

1) **You should ...**
   「〜した方がよい」という強い提案の意味で使います。
2) **had better + 動詞の原型** （should とは使う場面が異なります）
   「〜した方がよい（でないと罰がおきる）」というような、かなり脅迫的・強制的な表現であり、父親が子どもに諭すような場面で使います。

他にも「〜してはどうか？」という以下のような表現もあります。
   How about ... (ing) ?
   Why don't you ... ?
   What about ... ?
   Why not ... ?

★ アドバイスをするときは、なぜそのようにした方が良いのか、理由等を添えると良いでしょう。

Unit 1
Color

Dialogue 1   Logo and Background Colors

A: The contrast between red and green makes the logo stand out, but the halation makes it kind of difficult to look at.
B: What about reducing the saturation to balance the colors?
A: Another option might be to adjust the gradation.
B: But we should consider the ratio of the logo and the background.
A: Over here, the gray against the white background projects a calm feeling, but the logo doesn't really stand out.
B: By reducing the lightness, it will increase the contrast between the two colors, don't you think?

Q1: What are A and B suggesting?
Q2: What kind of suggestions would you give to improve the logo?

Unit 1
Color

Dialogue 2   Color Unity

 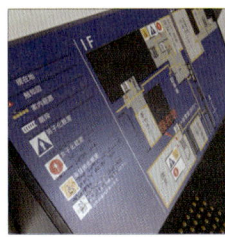 

A: Color unity is an important factor in sign planning, but I think yellow should be used for warnings to draw attention to them.

B: How about using the corporate color navy blue in the background?

A: Sounds good. That way we can keep the overall color unity, while improving the visibility.

B: What kind of typeface should we use?

A: Let's use one that is easy to read at a distance.

Q1: Why are they using yellow and navy blue?
Q2: What other colors would you use and why?

Unit 1
Color

Dialogue 3   Color Composition of a Garden Area

A: The overall image is dominated by the gray of the concrete. That could be because neutral colors bring together the overall color scheme.

B: Adding a little shade might make it better, don't you think?

A: Now that you mention it, the area with earth-green colors is small, but it tightens up the entire image.

B: By using the campus colors for the sign, we will also be able to accentuate the image.

....

Q: What are they suggesting to make the color composition look better?

Unit 1
Color

Dialogue 4 Body Color

A: Depending on how the color is applied, the look of this car will be completely different.

B: Yes. I used the new shiny materials for the promotional colors to make it look vibrant. In contrast, I chose colors that don't glare for the basic color line-up to make the car blend in better in the city.

A: Both colors have a certain character, and the material coloring matches well, doesn't it?

....

Q1: What do you think about using shiny materials for the promotional colors? How does it differ from using basic colors?

Q2: What color and materials would you use for this car?

15

Unit 1
Color

Dialogue 5 Workshop Color Scheme

A: The deep color of the wood makes it look a little heavy, but the gray part brings it all together to give it an overall cool impression, doesn't it?

B: The exposed part of the air conditioning duct matches the color of the ceiling, right?

A: Because the entire color scheme of the interior projects a calm feeling, it creates a very motivating space. I wonder if it was planned this way?

Q: What do you think of the color scheme projecting from the room in the picture?

Column　　彩度と発色

日本語でも混同しがちな彩度（**saturation**）と発色（**brilliance**）。**saturation** は色の三要素のうちの一つである彩度、つまり、一番無彩色から遠く鮮やかな度合を意味します。**brilliance** も大変よく似ていますが、発色や輝度の高さを表現するとき、例えば、光沢感や光輝性を持つ素材を形容するときやインクの発色の高さを表現するときに使います。また、非常にポジティブな意味を含みます。

This red should be changed to a higher color **saturation**.

Trees are **brilliant** green every spring.

It is a **brilliant** idea!

Column　　シンボルマークは和製英語？

日本でよく耳にするシンボルマークは、和製英語です。英語では、**mark** や **symbol** あるいは、**logo** や **logomark** などと表現します。厳密には、**logotype** は文字だけで構成されたものであり、**logomark** はそのブランドを象徴するマークだけで構成されたものです。

また、シンボルは、"The emperor is the **symbol** of Japan." というように象徴を意味しますので、**logomark** の方が一般的な表現のようです。

Column　　ハレーションは使わない？

色彩構成で、補色を隣同士に並べたとき、よく「ハレーションが起きる」と言いますが、**halation** という言葉はあるものの、実際にはあまり使わないようです。
「コントラストが強すぎる」や「オーラのようなものが出ている」などと表現するのだとか。

Column　　Character Color は日本語？

デザインを検討しているときに、製品のイメージコンセプトを表現するための主軸になる色をキャラクターカラーやメインカラーと言いますが、英語では何と表現しているのでしょうか？
実は、デザイン検討のステージでは特に決まった言い方はなく、以下のような表現が使われているようです。
communication color, brochure color, main color for advertising, hero color, character color
広告や営業に関わるコミュニケーションでは、**communication color** や **brochure color** が使われ、日本企業とのデザイン検討のやりとりでは、**character color** も使われるそうです。アメリカでは、**hero color** なんて言うこともあるそうですよ。

Unit 2
Form

この章では、具体的な形状や形のイメージについて検討する
ための表現を学習します。

Unit 2
Form

Keywords

Dg-1	**narrow** (v)	細くなる
Dg-1	**ridges** (n)	でこぼこ
Dg-2, 3	**taper/reverse taper** (n)	テーパー・逆テーパー
Dg-5	**gentle curve** (n)	緩やかな曲線
Dg-5	**smooth undulation** (n)	滑らかなうねり
Dg-5	**sloping** (adj)	傾斜した
Dg-6, 8	**overpowering** (adj)	圧迫感のある
Dg-7	**cross-section** (n)	断面
Dg-7	**surface layout** (n)	面構成

Useful Phrases

Dg-1	**If I can nitpick a little,**	欲を言えば
Dg-2	**I've tried to …**	〜しようとした
Dg-3	**At first glance,**	一見
Dg-6	**go for …**	（意図をもって）〜を試みる
Dg-6	**slit that separates it into two parts**	スリットを入れて2つの部分に分ける
Dg-7	**I don't know about that.**	それは、どうかな。
Dg-7	**Do what you think is best.**	好きにしなよ。

Unit 2
Form

Speaking Point 1

こだわり（目的や理由）についてを話すときには、以下のような表現が使えます。

1) **There is/are ... to ...**
   There is a bridge between the legs **to** strengthen it.
2) **It is important to ... so ...**
   It's important to have breaks at appropriate intervals **so** that the shoes don't get misshapen.
3) **I have put ... to ...**
   I've put in a slit **to** separate it.

Speaking Point 2

要望について話すときには、以下のような表現が使えます。

- **I want to (would like to) 動詞の原型 ... to ...**
   I wanted to use simplicity **to** express a sense of floating.

   ★ would を使うと丁寧になります。

   I want + 名詞
   hope to + 動詞の原型
   I'd rather + 動詞の原型

Unit 2
Form

Dialogue 1   Dryer Mock-up

A: Overall, it's simple and well put together.
B: Yes, it is. I especially like the graceful way the line **narrows** towards the opening.
A: **If I can nitpick a little,** is it possible to make the handle shape easier to grip?
B: I don't want to change the shape so how about putting in **ridges**?
A: I think doing that will ruin the simple shape.

Q: What are they talking about changing?

Unit 2
Form

Dialogue 2   Unconventional Stool Design

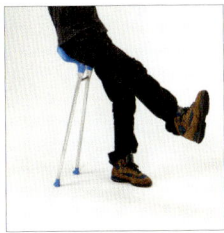

A: With the two legs it's kind of a casual design, huh?
B: The tapered legs give it even more of a sense of lightness.
A: How about strength? Does it feel stable when you sit down?
B: Yeah, that's no problem. There's a bridge between the legs to strengthen it and the seat is thicker. Our image is of something with weight so I've tried to highlight the sharp edges on the parts with volume.

Q: What is special about this chair?

Unit 2
Form

Dialogue 3   Improving a Table

A: It has a kind of lightness to it with the taper, doesn't it?
B: It'll be fun to look at when the thin trays come out.
A: Yeah, but it actually gives the impression of being unstable.
B: I've put in a reverse taper at the end of the pedestal to give it more stability.
A: At first glance, it looks like the four layers seemingly float.
B: Yes, I was trying to express a sense of floating and lightness.

Q: What do you like about this table? What do you dislike? Why?

Unit 2
Form

Dialogue 4   New Packaging Approach

A: It's a fresh new idea breaking away from the preconception of shoes coming packaged in a box.

B: I've thought of a way to wrap up footwear that can be used with shoes of any size.

A: Being able to see the soles lets us know what's inside right away, so it's a nice way to combine energy-savings with functionality.

B: And the flexible packaging forms around the shape of the shoes.

A: It's even possible to stack them and the simple form expresses a sense of fun. I think it's a great packaging idea for casual kid's shoes.

Q: What are the advantages of using this package?

Unit 2
Form

Dialogue 5   The Efficiency of Curves

A: The low-rise section of the roof has a gentle curve with a smooth undulation, giving an impression of suppleness.
B: Does the undulation affect the shape of the room?
A: The indoor ceiling is curved and the rooftop looks like waves gently lapping against a green hill.
B: It must be a strange and mysterious feeling standing in a sloping garden in the sky.

Q: What is special about the roof?

Unit 2
Form

Dialogue 6   Outer Wall Features

A: The smooth shape of most high-rise buildings makes them appear overpowering. I tried to change that with this building.
B: What exactly were you going for with this design?
A: I put in a slit that separates it into two parts. The outer wall and the balcony have extensions that protrude out.
B: The unevenness of the outer wall makes it look as if it were carefully pleated.
A: By slightly tilting the outer wall, your line of sight is shifted off of the other buildings.

Q: Describe the uniqueness of the outer wall.

Unit 2
Form

Dialogue 7 Car Model Form

A: Basically, the cross-section is quite strong and has a sense of solidity.

B: Yeah, but there is something that makes the surface layout not look right.

A: Too many elements around the face make it look busy. I think you should clean that up.

B: I don't know about that. I think having lots of strong elements is popular nowadays.

A: Okay. Do what you think is best.

....

Q: What is A suggesting?

Unit 2
Form

Dialogue 8   An Open Feel

A: The instrument panel is kind of overpowering.
B: Really? I think it gives off a sense of security.
A: It needs to have more of an open feel.
B: Okay, I'll think about making changes to the draft.

Q: What kind of suggestions would you give to B?

Column　　エッジ（端部）の表現も状況次第

デザインをする際に、ものの端部に気を付けることは重要な場合が多いですね。その際、「端部」や「エッジ」、「先」など、無意識に言葉を使い分けていると思いますが、これを英語で表現する場合、大きさや形、状況によって、表現が変わることを理解しておきましょう。

鉛筆の先のように点状の端部は **at the tip of** ...、テーブルの端部のように面状の端部（終わり）は **at the edge of** ...、一方、同じテーブルの端部でも角の部分であれば **at the corner of** ... を使います。

ところで、線の始めは **at the beginning of the line**、線の終わりは **at the end of the line** で表現できますが、**end of the line** は終電がなくなることも意味するので日常生活で使う際は気を付けましょう。

また、**tip of** ... は、もうすぐそこまで出かかっているのに、思い出せないときにも使います。
It's on the **tip of** my tongue!
こちらのほうが頻繁に使うかもしれませんね。

Unit 3
Material

この章では、各種素材について検討するための表現を学習します。

Unit 3
Material

Keywords

Dg-1, 5 **plating** (n)　メッキ加工

Dg-1, 7 **shiny** (adj)　光沢のある

Dg-1, 3 **transparent** (adj)　透明感のある

Dg-2　**diecast aluminum** (n)　アルミのダイキャスト

Dg-2　**blow molding** (n)　ブロー成形

Dg-2　**wrapped cloth** (n)　布巻(状態)

Dg-3　**solid wood** (n)　無垢材

Dg-3　**acrylic** (adj)　アクリルの

Dg-4　**corrugated cardboard** (n)　段ボール

Dg-4　**cardboard** (n)　ボール紙

Dg-7　**rough** (adj)　ザックリとした

Useful Phrases

Dg-2　**I'm not sure yet.**　今、悩んでいるところです。

Dg-2　**Don't you think that's a little unfashionable?**　野暮ったくないですか？

Dg-3　**cost distribution**　コスト（配分）

Dg-4　**expressive**　表情がある

Dg-5　**In addition,**　他にも、さらに

Dg-6　**comfortable cloth padding**　肌触りの良い布張り

Unit 3
Material

Speaking Point

説明するときには、利点と欠点を言いましょう。両方をバランスよく話すことで、説得力が増します。

1) **Although S + V, S + V**

   Although shoes usually **come** in a rectangular cardboard box, **using this kind of packaging gives** the impression of higher quality.

2) **Even though S + V, S + V**

   Even though the shoes were expensive, **he bought** them anyway.

3) **The best (worst) thing about it is ...**

   The best thing about my new job **is** that the people are really fun to work with.

4) **The trouble is ...**

   I like your new jacket. **The trouble is**, I don't think it will be warm enough in winter.

Unit 3
Material

Dialogue 1 Character and Use

A: The body is made of plastic, but I want to use chrome plating around the duct.

B: That leaves a rather cold impression. Couldn't we give it more warmth by using a different material? How about wood?

A: That might burn. Besides, I kind of imagined a cool breeze, so I wanted to use a shiny or transparent material.

B: How about the grip then? If the surface is too smooth, it might be slippery.

A: I was planning to put graining on the surface to avoid slipping.

Q: What other material could be used for the body and the grip?

Unit 3
Material

Dialogue 2   Aptitude and Possibility

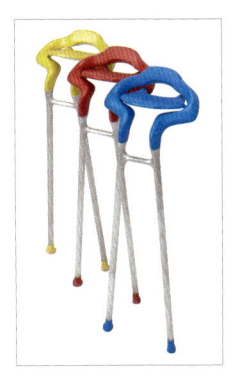

A: Are these legs going to be made from **diecast aluminum**?
B: **I'm not sure yet.** I was thinking of using titanium or carbon, because I want to make it as light as possible.
A: Don't you think that will raise the cost too high? Anyway, what material will you use for the seat?
B: I want to use a **blow molding** of ABS resin and then apply a finishing coat.
A: People are going to be sore from sitting on that. What about using a softer material like silicon or **wrapped cloth**.
B: **Don't you think that's a little unfashionable?**

....

Q: What material would you use for the legs and the seat?

Unit 3
Material

Dialogue 3   Choice and Cost

A: Using laminated wood for the material suggests a very casual type of furniture.
B: It's a lot cheaper compared to solid wood.
A: You used acrylic columns to keep the spaces between the boards?
B: Yes, I didn't want to draw any attention to anything but the boards themselves, so I used a material that was strong but transparent.
A: Don't you think acrylic is a little expensive?
B: Since, the main part is made from inexpensive laminated wood, I think the overall cost distribution is appropriate.

Q: What are other advantages and disadvantages of using acrylic columns?

Unit 3
Material

Dialogue 4   Choice and Benefits

A: I used corrugated cardboard for the packaging because it is soft and can be folded to fit different sizes and shapes for children's shoes.

B: It is a good idea. The material is strong yet expressive. Although shoes usually come in a rectangular cardboard box, using this kind of packaging gives the impression of higher quality.

A: Thank you. What's more, I think this flat but bendable material gives it an overall light feeling.

Q: How is this design better than a rectangular cardboard box?

Unit 3
Material

Dialogue 5   Building Materials

A: The structural frame is made of exposed concrete and the outer wall is finished with ribbed cement paneling.
B: The ribbing is very finely detailed which demonstrates its factory-made precision.
A: In addition, the silver aluminum canopy and the handrail finished with galvanized plating are a good combination of texture and materials.
B: It looks like they were thinking about durability as well.

Q: Explain the materials used for this building.

Unit 3
Material

Dialogue 6   Interior Materials

A: The combination of painted boards and wood paneling in the lecture hall interior leaves an impression that is calm and welcoming.

B: Was the wood wall using wood paneling designed utilizing joints?

A: Actually, the joints aren't being emphasized. It's the surface and the opening that are more prominent.

B: What kind of materials were used for the seats?

A: The armrests and back are made out of hardwood, and the rest of the seat is covered in comfortable cloth padding.

B: The wooden parts of the walls and chairs were all finished with the same dark colors, which gives a sense of unity.

....

Q: What do you think of the wooden walls? Do you think they match the overall interior design?

Unit 3
Material

Dialogue 7 Seat Materials

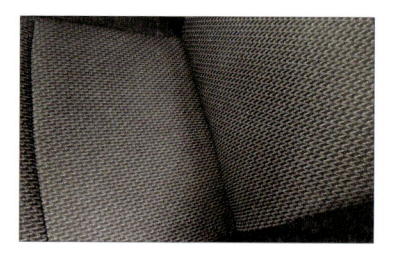

A: At first glance, this covering appears gray, but if you look closely you can see shiny threads that accent the color.
B: The rough texture is nice, too.
A: I think we should recommend using this high-quality brushed material to the sales department.

Q: What other material options can you think of for this chair?

Unit 4
Operation

この章では、動作や操作について検討するための表現を学習します。

Unit 4
Operation

Keywords

Dg-1	**rotate** (v)	回転させる
Dg-1	**horizontally** (adv)	水平に
Dg-1	**vertically** (adv)	垂直に
Dg-1	**balance** (n)	バランス
Dg-2, 3	**position** (n)	位置
Dg-2	**push** (v)	押す
Dg-2	**adjust** (v)	調節する
Dg-2	**press** (v)	押す
Dg-3	**shape** (n)	形
Dg-3	**pour** (v)	注ぐ
Dg-4	**lines of sight** (n)	視線
Dg-4	**stop and hang out** (v)	滞留する
Dg-5	**open** (v)	開け放つ

Useful Phrases

Dg-1	**By the way,**	ところで、
Dg-1	**You can ...**	〜してもよい
Dg-1, 2	**how do you ... ?**	〜どうするの？
Dg-4	**move from A to B**	AからBへと移動する
Dg-5	**Can you go ...**	〜へ出られる
Dg-5	**Being able to come and go**	出入りができる

Unit 4
Operation

Speaking Point 1

By the way, は、今まで話していたことと全く関係のない話をする場合の接続詞として使います。

A: I like the way you've adjusted the shape of the handle.

B: Thanks.

A: **By the way**, what do you think of the color scheme?

B: I like the balance among the colors.

他にも以下の表現が使えます。

Incidentally,

Speaking of which ...

You know ...

Speaking Point 2

How do you ...? は、「どのように~しますか？」または「どうやってしますか？」というように手段を尋ねるときに使えます。

A: I like the atmosphere of the open space between the buildings.

B: It can be bustling when there are lots of students around.

A: **How do you** get from one building to the other?

B: There are walkways on the second and fourth floors.

Unit 4
Operation

Dialogue 1   A Rotating Handle

A: By the way, how do you hold this hair dryer?
B: You can hold it like this and you can also rotate the handle.
A: You can rotate it horizontally? Or vertically?
B: In the picture it's rotated vertically.
A: Doesn't it throw off the balance if you hold it like that?

Q: What does A criticize about this design?

Unit 4
Operation

Dialogue 2   Position of the Button

A: I can't figure out how to use this drill. You push this button while holding it, right? But how do you adjust the drill speed?
B: I'm thinking of making a sliding button.
A: Wouldn't that be dangerous if it slipped? Why not put the start button on the bottom? You can select the drill speed on top and then start it by pressing the button.
B: Thank you, I'll think about that.

Q: What will B consider after hearing A's advice?

Unit 4
Operation

Dialogue 3   Getting Feedback

A: The position of the handle makes a beautiful shape, but don't you think it'll require quite a bit of strength when pouring the hot water?
B: Yeah, that's right. It may be better if it's supported at the bottom a little more.
A: Did you check to see if water drips out of the spout?
B: Not yet. I'm going to do that next.

Q: What problem does A mention?

Unit 4
Operation

Dialogue 4   Use of a Walkway

A: The outside walkway is really lively, isn't it?
B: That's because people use it when moving from classroom to classroom.
A: The quad is designed for people to circulate around, offering several lines of sight and encouraging activity.
B: There's also a place to stop and hang out, where you can ask teachers questions and things like that.

Q: According to A, what is the outside walkway designed to do?

Unit 4
Operation

Dialogue 5   A Sense of Openness

A: Can you go outside from this glass door?
B: Yeah. But you can't open the windows on either side of the door.
A: Opening the windows would give it a better sense of openness.
B: Being able to come and go freely would give a real sense of unity between the interior and exterior.

Q: According to B, what would happen if people could come and go freely?

Unit 4
Operation

Dialogue 6   Car View

A: With the pillar this wide, doesn't it make it hard to see out the back diagonally?
B: I think it needs to be like this in order to differentiate it from the competition.
A: I'll check the specifications of the competition to compare it as a benchmark.
B: If we want to make it thinner, we will have to negotiate with the designer.

Q: How does B defend the design?

Column　　いろいろな操作

「スイッチを操作する」には、その動作や状況に応じていろいろな言い方があります。

例えば、**knobs**、**buttons**、**handles**、**switches**、**dials** ですが、これらの名詞は操作するときの動作によって、それぞれ異なった動詞と組み合わせます。

knobs, handles: turn
buttons: push or press
switches: flip
dials: turn or twist

turn a knob: ノブを回す場合に使います。

turn on/off: つまみをひねってつける／消す、あるいは栓をひねって出す／止める場合に使います。

turn up/down: つまみをひねって音量などを上げる／下げる場合に使います。

push or press: ボタンなどを押す場合に使いますが、**press** は、ぐっと押し込んだり、押し続ける場合に使います。

flip a switch スイッチを指で軽くはじく場合に使います。

他にもどんな操作があるか考えてみましょう。

Unit 5
Composition

この章では、構成について検討するための表現を学習します。

Unit 5
Composition

Keywords

Dg-1, 5 **composition** (n)   構成
Dg-1   **contrast** (v)   対比する
Dg-1   **organized** (adj)   まとまっている
Dg-3   **courtyard** (n)   中庭
Dg-5   **symmetrical** (adj)   左右対称的な
Dg-5   **asymmetrical** (adj)   非対称的な
Dg-6   **work** (v)   効く
Dg-6   **geometric** (adj)   幾何学的な

Useful Phrases

Dg-1   **give it a twist**   パンチの効いた
Dg-2   **be aligned with ... in the center**   ～をセンター合わせにする
Dg-2   **farther away from ... rather than having them together**
       固めて配置するより～から離した方が
Dg-2   **look too crowded**   (要素が多過ぎて)ビジーになる
Dg-3   **be surrounded by ...**   ～で囲まれている
Dg-3   **be connected by ...**   ～で連結される

Unit 5
Composition

Speaking Point

I like how you ... は、褒め言葉に使える表現です。

1)「〜という点がいいですね。」

　　A: I think the accent isn't so good.

　　B: No, the accent is good. **I like how you**'ve done that.

　　A: Do you think so?

　　B: Yeah, it looks great.

2) 一旦褒めておいてから批判する場合にも使えます。

　　A: What do you think of the contrast?

　　B: **I like how you** did that but it may be a little too strong.

Unit 5
Composition

Dialogue 1   Overall Composition

A: I like how you used black. It contrasts well with the white part. Why don't you add the logo?
B: I think it is well organized as it is. Adding the logo might affect the balance.
A: Since it is monotone, why don't you use red to give it a twist.
B: Hmmm.

Q: Why doesn't B want to add the logo?

Unit 5
Composition

Dialogue 2   Logo Placement

A: I think the logo should be aligned with the switch in the center.
B: I would keep the logo farther away from the switch rather than having them together.
A: Right. It might look too crowded if you added "on and off" lettering.

Q: What does A suggest? Do you think it is a good idea?

Unit 5
Composition

Dialogue 3   The Distribution of Buildings

A: What do you think about this layout of the buildings?
B: The classrooms are all together in the lower part of the smaller building. The courtyard is surrounded by buildings on the north and south.
A: The two buildings are connected by a glass-covered bridge that seems to be floating. Also, there are external corridors that expand in three dimensions around the courtyard, which makes it easier for people to come and go.
B: Right. So where are the offices?
A: They're all located on the upper floors of the taller building. I think the layout accentuates the entire structure. The buildings are planned according to their purpose, so it is easy to understand.

Q: How are the two buildings joined together?

Unit 5
Composition

Dialogue 4   Model Improvement

A: This plan is generally well structured.
B: Yes. It looks really nice!
A: Do you have any ideas to improve on it?
B: Well, there are a few too many distracting details, so let's try rearranging it a little.

Q: What is the problem with this plan?

Unit 5
Composition

Dialogue 5   Symmetrical Composition

A: I like it. The symmetrical compositions are clear.
B: Do you think so? It seems a little dull to me. I think it might be better if it were asymmetrical.
A: No, it looks cool. The composition and the chic colors highlighted in black give it a real Japanese feel.
B: I see.

Q: Does A want to change this composition? Why or why not?

Unit 5
Composition

Dialogue 6   Intuitive Operation

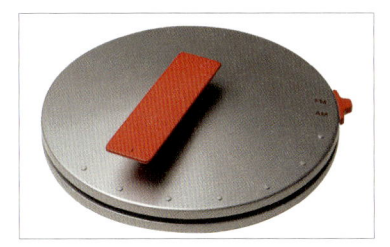

A: Having all the operating parts in red helps make using it intuitive. The red aluminum stain works well.
B: But the material leaves a little bit of a cold impression; as does the geometric shape.
A: Do you think so? To me it looks clean and beautiful. I think the lever positioned radially on the slightly curved surface makes it look elegant.

Q: What parts of this design does A think are good?

Column　　どのくらい下の方にある？

ある物がある物の下方にある場合に使える表現はいくつかありますが、それぞれ、関係や距離感が違います。さて、「猫がベッドの下にいる」下記の表現の違いをみてみましょう。

1) The cat is **underneath** the bed.
2) The cat is **under** the bed.

1)の場合、猫が姿が見えないほどベッドの下の奥に入り込んでいますが、2)は、猫は単にベッドの下にいるだけで、姿は見えています。
その他、下方を表現（イメージ）するものにも、状況によってさまざまな表現がありますので、使い分けに留意しましょう。

below：　　何か基準にするものと比較して、下にある場合

　　　　　　　She wore a skirt that fell **below** her knees.
　　　　　　　（彼女のスカートの丈は膝下だった。）

embedded：　埋めこまれている場合（下方とは限らない）

　　　　　　　The safe was **embedded** into the wall.
　　　　　　　（食器棚が壁に埋め込まれていた。）

　　　　　　　The telephone pole was **embedded** into the ground.
　　　　　　　（電柱は地面に埋め込まれていた。）

では、地下の部屋を表現するのはどうでしょうか。
単に、「1階の下にある」ということであれば、

The storage room is **below** the 1st floor.

もっとわかりやすく、「地下1階にある」のであれば、

The storage room is in the **basement**.
と言ってしまっていいでしょう。

Unit 6
Sense

この章では、イメージや感じたことを説明するための
表現を学習します。

Unit 6
Sense

Keywords

- Dg-1 **soothing** (adj)　和む、和らげる
- Dg-1 **intimidated** (adj)　怖い印象を持つ
- Dg-1 **cute** (adj)　かわいい
- Dg-1 **furry** (adj)　ふさふさの、毛でおおわれた
- Dg-1 **friendlier** (adj)　より親しみやすい
- Dg-2 **friendly** (adj)　親しみのある
- Dg-2 **elegant** (adj)　洗練された
- Dg-3 **advanced** (adj)　先進的な
- Dg-4 **openness** (n)　開放感
- Dg-4 **bustling** (adj)　活気のある

Useful Phrases

- Dg-2 **projecting an image that ...**　〜というイメージにした
- Dg-2 **you were going for ...**　〜な感じを求めた
- Dg-2 **(It) was the image that we had in mind.**　〜をイメージした
- Dg-3 **Wow!**　うわぁ！
- Dg-3 **... feel (advanced feel, cool feel)**　〜な感じ（先進的、かっこいい）
- Dg-3 **The way it is now**　このまま
- Dg-4 **calm and quiet**　静かで落ち着いた

Unit 6
Sense

Speaking Point 1

the way it is now is good は、「今のままが良い／今のままで良い」という意味であり、デザイン開発の途中段階でよく使う表現の一つです。

A: I think I should make the curved part straighter.

B: No, **the way it is now is good**.

A: You think so?

B: Yeah, it looks great.

他にも **it's fine as it is** などの表現もあります。

A: Do you think the image is too harsh?

B: No, **it's fine as it is** now.

A: Really?

B: Yeah. Don't change a thing.

Unit 6
Sense

Speaking Point 2

the image that we had in mind は「～をイメージした」というように、イメージしたことを表現するときに便利な表現です。

A: I like the gentle shape of the handle.

B: **The image we had in mind** was a soft stuffed animal.

A: That's exactly what it reminds me of.

他にも **I was going for** などの表現もあります。

A: What were you going for with this design?

B: **I was going for** an elegant space.

A: I can see that. It does have a calm and quiet feel to it.

Unit 6
Sense

Dialogue 1   Targeting Females

A: This shape has kind of a soothing appeal, doesn't it?
B: Yes. Women can be intimidated by electric drills. So we chose a shape like a small cute furry animal. We hope that this design will be thought of as friendlier.
A: So ... . it's a mole?
B: Yes. We thought it was appropriate because drills make holes, as do moles.

Q: Why did B introduce a mole as a motif for the drill?

Unit 6
Sense

Dialogue 2 Choosing a Certain Shape

A: Because it is a product that is commonly found in most homes, we thought that a design based on a small animal would be friendly, while at the same time projecting an image that is simple yet elegant.

B: So, you were going for a rooster?

A: Yes, getting up early to prepare the morning tea was the image that we had in mind.

Q: Why did A introduce a rooster as a motif for the kettle?

Unit 6
Sense

Dialogue 3   Cool Styling

A: Wow! This is super cool!
B: Actually, I wasn't going for such an advanced feel. I wanted something a little more loose and gentle.
A: The way it is now is really new and fresh. I've never seen anything like it anywhere!

Q: How does B feel about this car?

Unit 6
Sense

Dialogue 4   Versatility of Space

A: The rooftop with lots of greenery is very relaxing and has a real feeling of openness.
B: It's great, isn't it? The benches make it a place where we can really relax.
A: It's very calm and quiet now, but it will be busy when there are events taking place.
B: When my grandmother visited, she said it was a really lively place.
A: It's open to the public, with many people coming and going. At times it is bustling with activity.

Q: What are two reasons why A likes the rooftop?

Unit 7
Scale

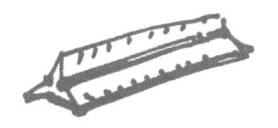

この章では、寸法や縮尺、スケール感に関する表現を学習します。

Unit 7
Scale

Keywords

Dg-1 **dimensions** (n) 寸法
Dg-1, 2 **half-scale** (adj) 2分の1スケール（2分の1の縮尺）の
Dg-1 **mock-up drawing** (n) モック図
Dg-1, 4 **drawing** (n) 図面
Dg-1, 4 **full-scale** (adj) 実物大の、原寸の
Dg-3 **(the scale) match(es) ...** (v) ～となじむ（スケール感）
Dg-4 **down to the smallest detail** 細部に至るまで
Dg-4, 5 **actual size** 実際の大きさ
Dg-5 **a sense of scale** スケール感

Useful Phrases

Dg-1 **Would it be possible to ... ?** ～することはできるかな？
Dg-1 **That reminds me,** それで思い出した、そういえば
Dg-1 **mistake A for B** AをBと間違える
Dg-2 **it might be a good idea to ...** ～は良さそうだね。
Dg-3 **be designed to ...** ～するように設計（計画）されている
Dg-3 **blend into ...** (v) ～にとけこむ（なじむ）
Dg-5 **It doesn't look like it.** そうは見えないよ。

Unit 7
Scale

Speaking Point 1

何かを依頼するときには、表現によって強制力が違ってくるので、使い分けを意識すると良いでしょう。

1) **Would it be possible to ... ?** は、丁寧な依頼として、「〜することはできますか（可能ですか）？」と尋ねる場合に使う表現です。

    A: **Would it be possible to** make a full-scale model?

    B: Yeah, I can do that.

2) より強い依頼の場合は、**You should ...** を使います。

    A: **You should** make a full-scale model.

    B: Okay, I can do that.

Unit 7
Scale

Speaking Point 2

デザインの意図を説明／質問しましょう。

1) **be designed (planned) to ...** は、「～となるように設計（計画）されている」といったように、デザイン意図を説明する際に便利な表現です。

   A: Why are the buildings all slightly different sizes?

   B: It **was designed to** look organic and not be too large.

2) デザインの意図を尋ねる場合は、**Why be ... designed (planned) ...?** を使います。

   A: **Why was** the open space **designed** in that shape?

   B: We wanted it to look inviting and relaxing.

Unit 7
Scale

Dialogue 1   Scale and **Dimensions**

A: Would it be possible to make a half-scale mock-up drawing of the coffee maker?
B: That shouldn't be a problem. Make sure you get the dimensions right!
A: That reminds me, did you ever order the mock-up of that coffee maker that could fit in one hand?
B: That is what I did, but I mistook the size of the half-scale drawings for full-scale when I ordered the mock-up.

Q: What is A reminded of in this dialogue?

Unit 7
Scale

Dialogue 2   Expressing Scale

A: I like the concept of this timepiece, but how big is it going to be?
B: About the size of a wristwatch.
A: Then it might be a good idea to make a sketch of someone using the watch, so that people can get an idea of the size.
B: Ok. I'll get my pencil. Do you want it in half-scale?
A: What? You'll draw it yourself and not use CAD?

Q: In order to comprehend the scale, what does A recommend?

Unit 7
Scale

Dialogue 3   Matching an Area's Environment

A: Even if the scale of the campus is big, the area of the building was designed to appear as if it doesn't take up a lot of space.
B: I read that the lower part of this building is divided into various sections, and the scale matches the neighboring residential area.
A: Yes, it's been designed so that the appearance of the building changes depending on the distance you view it from.
B: What do you mean?
A: The upper part of the building appears as a landmark from far away, but from closer up it blends into its surroundings.

Q: In what ways has the campus been designed to harmonize with its surroundings?

Unit 7
Scale

Dialogue 4   Safety Details

A: For the safety of the user, it should be planned carefully down to the smallest detail.
B: What kinds of things specifically?
A: For example, chamfering the concrete pillars. The actual size is about 1 cm, though.
B: The content has to be discussed using a full-scale model. What scale should we reduce the drawing to?

....

Q: Why do the designers have to plan carefully down to the smallest detail?

Unit 7
Scale

Dialogue 5   Sketching a Sense of Scale

A: I can't understand the sense of scale of the actual size of the car from this sketch.
B: I'm trying to draw a light vehicle.
A: It doesn't look like it. You should draw it by thinking about the balance between the body and the wheels.

Q: How does A suggest B should draw the sketch so that others can comprehend the scale?

Column　　何の大きさ？どんな大きさ？

big、**large**、**huge**、**great** は、どれも体積、面積、規模などが大きいことを表します。
big はどちらかというと主観的な表現に使用され、感情的な意味を含む表現に使われることもあります。
それに対して、**large** は一般的な形容詞として客観的に物理的な大きさや広さを表します。
例えば、large mouth は面積的に「大きな口」という意味ですが、big mouth は、同じ「大きな口」という意味の他に、「おしゃべり」や「大ぼら吹き」という意味でよく使われます。このような性質からか、**big** は話し言葉で使用されることが多く、書き言葉で使用されることが多いのは **large** です。

huge や **great** は対象となる物の大きさや事の程度が驚くほど大きい、または印象的である場合に使います。
huge は数量に対して使われることが多く、**great** は人の感情や経験に対してよく使われます。
huge space は広大な空間ですが、great space になると素晴らしい空間という意味になります。
ただし、Great Lakes や Great Barrier Reef の場合は、同種のものと比較して非常に大きいことを意味します。
great は形容詞を強調する副詞として使われることもあり、**big** と一緒に He has great big arms.（彼の腕は、ものすごく大きい。）などと使うこともあります。
ちょっとややこしいですが、面白いですね。

Unit 8
Situation

この章では、デザインの対象や使用状況・場所などに関する表現を学習します。

Unit 8
Situation

Keywords

- Dg-1 **in their 20's or 30's** 20代から30代の
- Dg-1 **amateur** (n) 初心者
- Dg-1 **do-it-yourself** DIY
- Dg-2 **senior** (n) 高齢者
- Dg-3 **be located near ...** (v) ～に隣接する
- Dg-3 **harmonize with ...** (v) ～と調和する
- Dg-3 **neighboring skyline** (n) 周辺のスカイライン
- Dg-3 **easy access** (n) アクセスのしやすさ
- Dg-4 **facing** (v) 面する

Useful Phrases

- Dg-1 **be aimed at ...** ～を想定している
- Dg-1 **be targeting ...** ～をターゲットにしている
- Dg-2 **Regarding ...** ～の件だけど、
- Dg-2 **I think so, too.** そうだね。
- Dg-2 **We need to make improvements** 改善が必要だ
- Dg-3 **placement in ...** ～に位置する
- Dg-4 **How is it used?** どのように使われている？
- Dg-4 **be intended for ...** ～を対象とした、～専用の

Unit 8
Situation

Speaking Point 1

使い方で意味が変わる単語に注意しましょう。
locate という動詞は、be 動詞を付ける場合と付けない場合で意味が違ってきます。

1) **be + located**（都市や街が「地図上などで」位置することを示す）

   Hamamatsu **is located** in Shizuoka Prefecture.

2) **locate**（≒ **find** みつける）

   I couldn't **locate** Hamamatsu on the map of Japan.

Unit 8
Situation

Speaking Point 2

賛成と反対の表現を身に付けましょう。

Agree（賛成）	— Disagree（反対）
Great idea!	— **That's a good idea, but maybe we should ...**
I think so too.	— **I'm not so sure about that.**
Ok. Let's do that.	— **How about instead we ...?/How about we try ...?**

★ ディスカッションでは、相手の意見に賛成や反対を唱える場合があり、その表現もさまざまです。
相手の意見に反対するときには、相手の気持ちを害さぬよう、表現に気を付ける必要があります。（日本語のときと同じですね）

Dialogue 1 A New Target User Concept

A: This tool is aimed at women in their 20's or 30's who like handmade crafts and amateurs who have a "do-it-yourself" attitude.

B: Isn't the "do-it-yourself" attitude supposed to be held by fathers and husbands?

A: We are targeting women who have begun living alone for the first time. If we make the tools look cool, then we hope that people will enjoy assembling furniture.

Q: What are some other ideas that could make this product more appealing to the target group?

Unit 8
Situation

Dialogue 2   Design Features and Conditions

A: Regarding the dial for the air conditioner, I think it may be too small to turn while driving.

B: I think so, too. We need to make improvements because many of the users will be seniors. How about making the letters on it glow in the dark?

A: That might work. What about using the digital display? It might be a little difficult for seniors to operate.

Q: How would the design needs of older drivers differ from younger ones?

Unit 8
Situation

Dialogue 3   Site Condition and Planning

A: One characteristic of this university is its placement in an urban area. It is located near an elementary school and a park, forming a zone of education and culture.
B: Do you think the campus harmonizes with the surrounding area?
A: Yes, the low-rise buildings match the neighboring skyline well. However, while the high-rise building is definitely a landmark in the area, it does stand out a little.
B: We can see that they were trying to create a friendly space by offering easy access to a campus full of lush greenery.

Q: What are the advantages of a university that is located near the city center?

Unit 8
Situation

Dialogue 4 Possible Uses of Space

A: There is a studio on the first floor of the southern part of the campus, facing near the road.
B: How is it used?
A: This room was intended not only for students, but also for members of the local community.
B: What generations of people would use it the most?
A: We imagined that active retirees would be most interested in conducting activities there.

Q: What kind of use is good for a room facing near the road?

Unit 9
Light and Shadow

この章では、光と影に関する表現を学習します。

Unit 9
Light and Shadow

Keywords

Dg-1   **permeate** (v)   透過する

Dg-1, 2 **shadow** (n)   影

Dg-1   **quantity of light** (n)   光量

Dg-1, 4 **shine** (v)   照らす

Dg-2   **cast** (v)   光、影などを投じる

Dg-2, 3 **sunlight** (n)   日差し

Dg-3   **reflection** (n)   反射、映り込み

Dg-4   **phosphorescent** (adj)   蛍光の、燐光を発する

Dg-5   **direct lighting** (n)   直接照明

Dg-5   **indirect lighting** (n)   間接照明

Dg-5   **diffuse** (v)   拡散する、普及する、流布する

Dg-5   **lit** (adj)   照らされた

Useful Phrases

Dg-1   **differ from ...**   〜と異なる

Dg-2   **pour into**   降り注ぐ

Dg-3   **the shape's intention**   カタチの意図

Dg-5   **the desired effect**   望まれる効果

Unit 9
Light and Shadow

Speaking Point 1

1) **image**

   日本語でよくイメージという言葉を使いますが、英語の **image** には幅広い意味があります。一般的な感覚を表現する場合だけでなく、画像を指す場合にも使います。

   - Wearing that leather jacket gives you a tough **image**.
   - Let's choose another **image** for the sample. This one is too dark.

   動詞（イメージする）として使う場合は、**imagine** を使います。

   - I can't **imagine** what the final product will look like.

2) **appearance**

   どのように見えるかを表現するときに用いる言葉ですが、特に外見に関する場合に使います。

   - His new earring gave him a youthful **appearance**.

   動詞として使う場合は，**appear** を使います。

   - I don't want to **appear** rude, but I really have to leave before 5 a.m.

image は心に描いた印象について、**appearance** は外見からの様子に使います。

Unit 9
Light and Shadow

Speaking Point 2

何らかの状況を表現する場合、目に見えるものには **look**、耳で聞いたことに対しては **sound** を使います。

1) **look**
   - **look** + 形容詞 — 何々に見える
     You **look tired**.
   - **look like** + 名詞 — 何々のように見える
     The clouds **look like cotton candy** floating in the sky.

2) **sound**
   - **sound** + 形容詞 — 話を聞いて、何々に見える、思う
     Your plan **sounds great**.
   - **sounds like** + 名詞 — 何々のように見える、感じる
     That **sounds like a great idea**!（電話中）

Unit 9
Light and Shadow

Dialogue 1   Lighting Effects

A: Light permeates through the material, creating a beautiful shadow.
B: Can you control the lighting conditions?
A: Yes. By adjusting the quantity of light and the angle of the lampshade, you can create the kind of shadow you want.
B: It would be okay to shine the light directly on the floor, but it could also come from the ceiling or the wall as well.

Q: How does natural light differ from artificial light?

Unit 9
Light and Shadow

Dialogue 2 — Creating Light and **Shadow**

A: I like the intricate shadow that the canopy casts on the wall.
B: That's because the canopy has several slits in it.
A: I see. It was made that way to disperse the sunlight coming in from the windows, creating a rhythmical shadow pattern on the outer wall.
B: It also controls the amount of light pouring into the room, creating a bright and comfortable space.

Q: What effect does the canopy have on the building?

Unit 9
Light and Shadow

Dialogue 3   Reflection and Car Surface

A: I tried to adjust the angle so that the light would highlight the shoulder better.
B: The reflection is beautiful, and we can easily understand the shape's intention.

Q: What factors do car designers need to consider concerning the reflection of sunlight on a car body?

Unit 9
Light and Shadow

Dialogue 4   Lighting and Readability

A: The position of this sign is so dark I can't read the lettering.
B: It has to be put somewhere that is bright enough to be able to read it. Many elderly people have cataracts, making it even more difficult to read. We have to consider that as well.
A: Okay then, how about shining a spotlight on it? Or making the panel itself shiny?
B: How about making the lettering out of phosphorescent materials?
A: Okay. Let's make a sample first and see how it looks.

Q: What are other ways to increase the visibility of the lettering?

Unit 9
Light and Shadow

Dialogue 5 Lighting Effects

A: It's interesting how direct and indirect lighting can have a completely different effect.
B: That's true. But even the same direct lighting can be concentrated or diffused to perform different functions.
A: That's why you have to put a lot of thought into the desired effect.
B: I see. For example, people need indirect lighting so that they can relax in the bath, but they also need direct lighting for doing things like shaving.
A: Or when a restaurant uses a brightly lit sign to attract customers.
B: Let's look at some other effects.

Q: According to the conversation, how can indirect lighting be used to perform a function?

Column　　きらきら？ぎらぎら？

輝いている様子を表現するとき、その輝き方によってさまざまな表現があります。

shiny は、磨かれた表面が反射して輝いているようなときに使います。太陽光や磨かれた物に反射した光のように、一定してそれ自身が放つ光を表現し、瞬くような光には使いません。
the **shiny** new car

一方、**twinkling** は星や遠方の灯火のようにキラキラと瞬くような光を表現します。また、**sparkling** は、火花のような一瞬の閃光を表現します。
The brightness of **twinkling** stars is stronger than **sparkling** stars.

glittering もキラキラとした光ですが、小さな破片に反射したような光を表現します。
The surface of the water **glitter**ed in the sunlight.

glaring は、ギラギラとした目が眩むような強い光を表現し、けばけばしい色という表現にも使います。
the **glaring** sun（強い太陽光）
pattern **glare**（錯視などによってパターンがちらちらする現象）

dazzling も目が眩むような強い光を表現しますが、うっとりするような雰囲気を含み、ポジティブな表現によく使われます。
dazzling diamonds
a **dazzling**ly beautiful woman

Unit 10
Function

この章では、機能、関連動作等について検討するための表現を学習します。

Unit 10
Function

Keywords

- Dg-1　**widen** (v)　拡大する、広げる
- Dg-1　**easy to use**　使いやすい
- Dg-2　**emphasize** (v)　強調する
- Dg-3　**fold** (v)　折りたたむ
- Dg-3　**store** (v)　収納する、保管する
- Dg-3　**hygiene** (n)　衛生
- Dg-4　**comfortable** (adj)　快適な、居心地のよい
- Dg-4　**act** (v)　〜として働きかける、〜になる

Useful Phrases

- Dg-1　**make it** (adj)　〜にする、となる
- Dg-1　**get dirty easily**　汚れやすい
- Dg-1　**be suitable for**　適した、ふさわしい
- Dg-2　**reduce the impact**　負荷を軽減する
- Dg-2, 4　**as well**（文尾で）　〜も、なおその上
- Dg-2, 3　**A as well as B**　BだけでなくAはもちろん
- Dg-3　**repeated use**　繰り返しの使用
- Dg-3　**That's true.**　確かに。
- Dg-4　**(be) immersed in**　没頭する、ふける

Unit 10
Function

Speaking Point

動詞＋接尾辞で形容詞に変化するケースでは、同じ動詞でも **+ed** か **+ing** で意味が違ってきますので注意が必要です。
次の例文で理解を深めましょう。

1) **+ed**（接尾辞）で形容詞となり、人の感情を表します。

 ★ 主語は人に限ります。

 - I was confus**ed** by the remote control because it has too many functions.
 - I was disappoint**ed** by the movie.
 - Scientists were surpris**ed** by the new research data.
 - I was really tir**ed** after climbing the stairs.

2) **+ing**（接尾辞）で形容詞となり状況を表します。

 - This remote control is confus**ing** because it has too many functions.
 - The movie was disappoint**ing**.
 - The new research data was surpris**ing**.
 - Climbing the stairs was really tir**ing**.

他にも以下のような例があります。
 bored/boring
 excited/exciting
 embarrassed/embarrassing

Unit 10
Function

Dialogue 1   Storage Space Materials

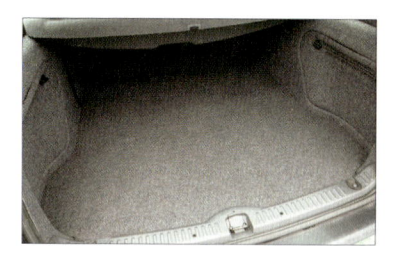

A: Widening the space for luggage made it easier to use, but despite the high cost, I think we should also have used materials that don't get dirty easily.
B: I think so too. Doing that will prevent user complaints. Let's consider that for next time.

Q: What do you think is suitable material for this space?

Unit 10
Function

Dialogue 2 — The Value of a Roof Garden Terrace

A: This is a large-scale roof garden terrace. Because it is hilly, it really emphasizes a natural environment.
B: Why did they make it this way? For environmental reasons?
A: Yes. By making it this way, they can really reduce the building's impact on the environment, such as the heat-island effect.
B: Does it have an effect on the interior of the building as well?
A: Yes, it can also reduce the impact of outside heat on the building.
B: So it is good for the building as well as the surrounding urban area!

Q: How should this roof garden terrace be maintained?

Unit 10
Function

Dialogue 3   Beverage Storage

A: After using it, this bag can be folded into a very compact size, so it can be stored easily.
B: Are there any problems? What about hygiene?
A: No. The opening can also be made wide, making it easy to put liquids in as well as clean. Also, if we make it out of silicon, it can be cleaned with hot water.
B: But there might be a chance that some liquids could stain the material, or repeated use could cause the opening to stretch.
A: That's true. Let's think it over.

Q: Why does A want to think it over?

Unit 10
Function

Dialogue 4   New Movie Theater

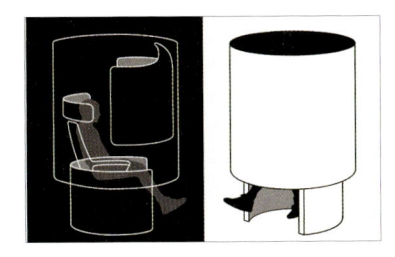

A: This is called a personal movie theater?
B: That's right. It functions like a regular movie theater, but you are free to enjoy the movie on your own.
A: It's different from watching a DVD at home because of the comfortable seat and high quality sound system, allowing the moviegoer to more easily become immersed in the story.
B: There are also larger models available, allowing two or more people to share in the experience as well.
A: The paneling on the outside booth would also display what movie is being watched, which acts as advertising.
B: That's right. Do you want to try it for yourself?

Q: What are the differences between this new kind of movie theater and a regular one?

Column　　仕様や特徴、性能を示すとき

仕様を示す「スペック」は、一言で片づけがちですが、種類に応じた英語表現を知っておくと便利です。

specifications（仕様）
standard specifications（標準仕様書）
performance specifications（性能仕様書）

その他に、特徴や性能を表現する言葉として、**features** や **qualities** という言葉がありますが、これらは、どのように使い分けるのでしょうか。具体的な物でイメージしてみましょう。

例えば、TV のリモコンの場合

specifications:　対応機種、使用距離・角度など（技術的なデータ）
features:　　　　ボタンがカラーでわかりやすいなど(特筆すべき特徴)
qualities:　　　　長方形状、プラスチック製など（見てわかる特性）

うまく使い分けて表現すれば、デザインを的確に説明することができますね。

Unit 11
Application

この章では、コンペティションに応募するための表現を学習します。

Unit 11
Application

Keywords

Cp-1, 2	**application requirements** (n)	応募要項
Cp-1, 2	**prize** (n)	賞
Cp-1	**entry category** (n)	募集対象
Cp-1	**eligibility** (n)	応募資格
Cp-1, 2	**judges** (n)	審査員
Cp-1, 2	**initial judging/first round screening** (n)	一次審査
Cp-1, 2	**final judging** (n)	最終審査
Cp-1	**judging criteria/screening criteria** (n)	審査基準
Cp-1	**marketability** (n)	商品化の可能性
Cp-1, 2	**entry** (n)	エントリー、登記
Cp-1	**results announcement** (n)	結果通知
Cp-1	**application documents** (n)	応募用紙
Cp-1	**personally identifiable information** (n)	個人を特定できる情報
Cp-2	**biography** (n)	略歴文、バイオグラフィー、伝記

Useful Phrases

Cp-2	**be majoring in …**	〜を専攻している
Cp-2	**have a particular interest in …**	特に〜に興味を持っている
Cp-2	**with a focus on …**	〜に焦点をあてて
Cp-2	**The goal of one's designs is …**	目指すデザインは〜

Unit 11
Application

Speaking Point

コンペティションへの応募では、しばしば略歴の記載が求められます。英語の略歴文では、自分のことを **author**、**he**、**she** などと第三者的に表現します。

また、ほとんどの場合、**word count**（単語数）に制限がありますので、注意しましょう。

Kaitou Yamada is a fourth-year student in the Faculty of Design at University of Art and Culture. **Mr. Yamada** is majoring in Industrial Design and has a particular interest in product design with a focus on Universal Design and making environmentally friendly products. **Mr. Yamada** has presented on **his** work at design conferences in Tokyo and Osaka. **He** hopes to be a product designer with a keen sense of the people and world around him. The goal of **Mr. Yamada's** designs is to help people have better lives that are in harmony with their surroundings. (95 words)

Unit 11
Application

Competition 1 Application Requirements

20th UAC Campus Goods Award

Theme: Gift items that foster knowledge and beauty
Intelligent and beautiful gift items that promote UAC

PRIZES: Grand Prize ¥1,000,000、 Category Award ¥100,000

CATEGORIES: Novelty, Merchandise

ENTRY CATEGORY: Stationery or other gift items

ELIGIBILITY: Any individual or group from a corporation, organization, regardless of age, sex, professional background, or nationality.
Entry eligibility is limited to those designs that have never been shown before publicly.

JUDGES: Bunta Shizuoka, Gate Hamamatsu, Umiko Sorada

JUDGING PROTOCOL: Initial judging / Based on presentation sheet
Final judging / Based on design model and panel

JUDGING CRITERIA: Suitability as a university gift item, portability, aesthetics, marketability

SCHEDULE:

Entry / October 1-November 1, 2016 (tentative)

Initial Judging / By end of November (Only successful entrants will be contacted).

submission for final judging / Must arrive on or before December 25, 2016. Final judging will be decided by panel and Design Model.

results announcement / Winners will be contacted directly and posted on the advertising website on February 1, 2017.

Unit 11
Application

Competition 1 Application Documents

Presentation Sheet for Initial Judging (Front)

Please do not put any personally identifiable information above the double line.

1. Title

   Tea Break (Bookmark)

2. Category

   Novelty item

3. Concept (Within 200 words)

   The bookmark is made of wood. It projects the image of tea leaves. The bookmark gives off a tea scent whenever the user puts it between pages. It makes users feel relaxed, as if they are drinking tea during a short break from reading.

===

Name: Mika Hama
Name of the Group (Not required for individual applications):
   ORANGE
Address: 11-11 Oka-ward, Matsuhama-city
E mail: mmt@uac.ac.jp
Profession: University student

Unit 11
Application

Presentation Sheet for Initial Judging (Back)

4. Figures: 3D-CG, Pictures of Models, Illustrations, etc.
   Include measurements that demonstrate the size of the object.

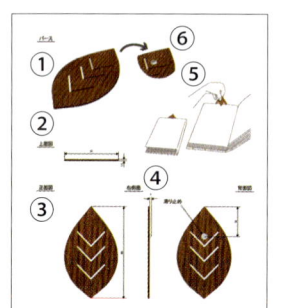

① Perspective
② Top view
③ Front view
④ Side view
⑤ Instructions on use
⑥ Slip stopper on the back side

Q. Before applying to a competition, make notes on the following things:

1. What kind of submission are they looking for?
   _____

2. When is the final submission deadline (due date)?
   _____

3. How is the initial judging done?
   _____

4. How is the final judging done?
   _____

5. How will applicants know the final results?
   _____

Unit 11
Application

Competition 2 Application Requirements

40th UAC City Award

Theme: Monument to enrich the downtown area
A plan to revitalize the downtown area

Sponsor: Machinaka Union of UAC city **Co-sponsor:** Geijutsu Inc.
Prizes: First Place (One from all entries) ¥ 2,000,000 and gift items
Second Places (Two from all entries) ¥ 300,000 each
Judges: Taro Yamada, Hanako Bungei, Ichiro Noguchi

First-round Screening
Registration: Applicants are required to pre-register. After registration via internet, applicant must send registration sheet to the host institution.
Submission of drawings: Floor plan, section, site plan (any scale allowed), perspective view or picture of model, notes or figures to explain the concept (within 100 words).
Materials: A2 (Complete all drawings, illustrations, and texts on one sheet of thick drawing paper.) Do not use panels.
Submission: Send the drawing with the registration sheet on the back by post. No hand-delivered (not by post) submissions will be accepted.

Schedule
Pre-registration: April 1 - April 15, 2016
Deadline: June 1, 2016 / Must be postmarked on or before the deadline.
Initial screening: Early July, 2016 Only successful entrants will be contacted.

Final Screening
Final screening interviews and presentations: Applicants who have passed the initial screening will receive a final judging of their work by open interview.
Announcement of final screening results: Winners will be announced in the Monthly "BUNKAGEIJUTSU", Vol.10, 2016.

Additional Information
· Works already published elsewhere will not be accepted.
· The sponsors will not answer questions regarding competition regulations.
· The entrant is responsible for all application costs for the contest.
· Works submitted will not be returned.
· Copyright for the winning entries will remain the property of the designers, but the sponsors of the competition reserve the right to publish the entries in magazines and other media.

Unit 11
Application

Competition 2 Submitting Documents

Requirement Information on Submission Paper for Initial Judging (1 Sheet, A2)

1. Entry Title
   Growing garden

2. Concept
   This is a proposal for a garden that grows with people over time. The site is located at the square entrance of a shopping area. The floor consists of circular stone plates floating on a pond. The garden grows over time and flowers bloom magnificently. According to the plan, the downtown area is bustling with activity thanks to the growth of the garden.

3. Diagram of the concept

4. Floor plan and Site plan (Scale/ 1:30)

5. Section (Scale/ 1:30)

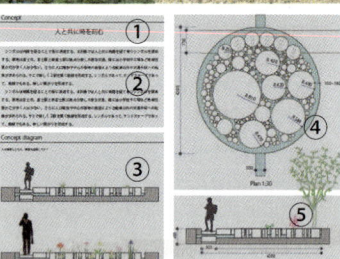

Unit 11
Application

Registration Sheet for Initial Judging (Attach to the back side)

Name (group representative)   Mika Hama
Workplace or School (Year)   University of Art and Culture (senior)
Age   22
Address   11-11 Oka-ward, Matsuhama-city
E-mail   mmt@uac.ac.jp

Designer's Biography (Within 100 Words)

Mika Hama is a senior student in the Faculty Design at University of Art and Culture. She is majoring in Spatial Design and has a particular interest in architecture with a focus on making environmentally friendly buildings. She received first prize at the SSS Space Award in 2014. The goal of Ms. Hama's designs is to help people have better lives that are in harmony with their surroundings.
(68 words)

Activities

Activities

Unit 1　Color

Activity 1　ベストドレッサー / Best Dresser

周囲を見まわして、一番素敵な色合わせの服装をしている人を選び、その理由を発表しましょう。

Look at someone around you, and choose who you think is wearing the best color-coordinated outfit. Explain why you chose this person.

1人で学習する人は、下の写真や雑誌などを見て、その色合わせの好きな点について説明してみましょう。

Instructions for individual study:

Look at the picture below or at pictures of people in a magazine and practice describing what you like about their color coordination.

Activities

How to Begin

〈 For pairs or groups 〉

Aのコーディネートが一番素敵だと思います。
I think the color coordination of person A is the best.

〈 For individuals 〉

彼女のコーディネートは良いと思います。その理由は……
I think her coordination is good, because ...

Activity Notes

〜と調和している / harmonize well with ...
〜とバランスがとれている / balance well with ...
〜が服装のコーディネートを引き締めている / be accentuated by ...
彼女を〜に見せている / make her look (adj.)

関連ユニット： Unit 5 Unit 6

Activities

Unit 1　Color

Activity 2　ロゴマーククイズ / Logo Mark Quiz

雑誌の中からロゴマークを選び、その形や色や構成についてパートナーに口頭で説明し、何のマークか当ててもらいましょう。

From a nearby magazine, choose some company logos and describe them in terms of shape, colors and overall composition to your partner. Have your partner try to guess what company each logo represents.

1人で学習する人は、下のロゴについて、電話で誰かに話すように説明してみましょう。

Instructions for individual study:

Look at the following logos and describe them as if you were explaining them to someone on the telephone. Check your explanations with the sample answer.

Logo 1

Logo 2

Logo 3

118

Activities

How to Begin

このマークは……

This mark is …

Activity Notes

下に / under, down, below, on the bottom
上に / upper, above, over, on the top
中心に / in the middle, in the center
前に / in front
後ろに / behind
右上に / upper right

関連ユニット：Unit 2　Unit 5

Activities

Unit 1 Color

Activity 3　ツートーンボディーカラー / Two-Tone Body Color

若手カラーデザイナーとベテランの生産技術担当者が、ボディーカラーのツートーン色について話しています。下の条件をもとに、この二人の会話を想定してロールプレイングをしてみましょう。

A young color designer and a veteran production engineer are talking about a two-tone body color. Role-play the scenario based on the information below.

- カラーデザイナーは数種類のツートーン塗装の開発をしたいと思っています。

  Color designers want to develop various types of two-tone body color schemes.

- 生産技術担当者は、現実的な問題点を挙げます。

  The production engineer points out some practical limitations.

デザイナーの立場で、生産技術担当者を説得してみましょう。

Try to persuade the production engineer about the car design from the perspective of a designer.

1人で学習する人も、デザイナーの立場での説得を考え解答例と比較してみましょう。

Instructions for individual study:
Check your explanation with the sample answer.

Activities

How to Begin

〈 For pairs or groups 〉

カラーデザイナー：…… について相談したいのですが。

Color designer: I'd like to talk about …

〈 For individuals 〉

私は……の理由で、数種類のツートーン塗装にしたいと思います。

I want to use various types of two-tone body color schemes, because ...

Activity Notes

カラーデザイナー / color designer

組み合わせ / combination

競合他社 / competitors

生産技術担当者 / production engineer

生産の都合上 / due to production technology

設備 / facility

やりくり / make it work

コスト / cost

関連ユニット： Unit 8

Activities

Unit 2　Form

Activity 4　ショールームでのやり取り / Give and Take at a Showroom

カーディーラーのショールームで店員と中年の女性客が、展示車について話しています。下の条件をもとに、この二人の会話を想定してロールプレイングをしてみましょう。

A middle-aged female customer talks with a salesperson about a display car in the showroom of the car dealer. Role-play the scenario based on the information below.

- 店員は、セールスポイント（新型車、デザインの特徴、LED ライト）について説明しています。

  The salesperson is explaining the sales points (new model, design characteristics, LED head light).

- 女性客は、自分の好み（色、形、大きさ）を店員に伝えています。

  A female customer is relating her preferences (color, shape, size) to a salesperson.

女性客にピッタリのクルマを勧めてみましょう。

Recommend a suitable car for the female customer, supplying reasons that you think she would find appealing.

1人で学習する人も、店員の立場で説明を考え解答例と比較してみましょう。
<u>Instructions for individual study:</u>
Check your explanation with the sample answer.

Activities

How to Begin

店員：こちらが発売されたばかりの ……

Salesperson: This car was just released …

Activity Notes

店員 / salesperson
先月発売の / just released last month
トレンド / a trendy fit
スポーティーな / sporty
ピッタリ / fit
女性客 / female customer
カワイイ / pretty
派手過ぎ / too showy
シートの柄 / seat pattern
色 / color

関連ユニット：Unit 1　Unit 8

Activities

Unit 3 Material

Activity 5　製品の素材 / Product Materials

製品に使用する素材について、良い点と悪い点を挙げて検討しましょう。
Let's look in more depth at the materials we use to make products. Consider both the strengths and weaknesses of each.

How to Begin

〜に対して (素材) を使ったら、どういう良い点がありますか？
What are the positives when (material) is used for ...?

1人で学習する人は、良い点と悪い点を書き出してみましょう。
Instructions for individual study:
Check your writing with the sample answer.

	皿 plates/dishes	
	長所 positives	短所 negatives
紙 paper		
プラスチック plastic		
陶器 pottery		
ガラス glass		
金属 metal		
その他 others		

Activities

Activity Notes

割安感のある / reasonable
安価な / inexpensive
安っぽい / cheap
割れやすい / fragile
履きやすい / wearable
汚れやすい / get dirty easily
購入しやすい / affordable
使い捨て（の）/ disposable
長持ちする / durable
蒸れる / sweat
質感 / texture quality

関連ユニット： Unit 1　Unit 2　Unit 4　Unit 5
　　　　　　　Unit 6　Unit 8　Unit 9　Unit 10

Activities

Unit 4 Operation

Activity 6　取り扱い説明 / Directions

商品カタログから選んだ製品の機能と使い方についてパートナーに説明し、何について説明しているのかを当ててもらいましょう。パートナーは説明後に質問できますが、あなたは Yes か No だけで答えましょう。

Describe a product from a paper or online shopping catalog in terms of its functions and how to use it. Have your partner guess what the product is. Your partner may ask questions about the product after your explanation, but you may only answer yes or no.

1人で学習する人は、下の製品について操作部の機能と使い方を説明し、解答例と比較してみましょう。

Instructions for individual study:

Describe each product in terms of its functions and how to use it. Compare your description with the sample answers.

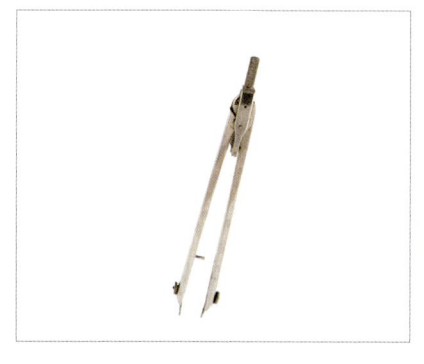

Activities

How to Begin

この製品を使うときには、まず……
When you use this product, first of all, …

Activity Notes

初めに / First,
次に / Next,
必要に応じて / as necessary
〜の場合は / In the case of …

関連ユニット：Unit 1　Unit 2　Unit 9　Unit 10

Activities

Unit 4 Operation

Activity 7　昔のテレビ / An Old TV

父親が見つけてきた古いテレビを息子が珍しそうに見ています。下の条件をもとに、2人の会話を想定してロールプレイングをしてみましょう。
A son looks curiously at an old TV found by his father. Make a dialogue between the father and son, then role-play the scenario with a partner based on the information below.

- 父親は、古いモノの良さを伝えようとしています。
  The father is talking about the advantages of older products.
- 息子は、新しいテレビの方が便利だと思っています。
  The son points out how much more convenient new products are.

1人で学習する人は、下の項目について昔のテレビと今のテレビの違いを説明してみましょう。
Instructions for individual study:
Compare and contrast the differences between old and modern TVs, concerning the following.

a) 電源スイッチ／ switches
b) チャンネル選択／ changing channels
c) 壊れたときの直し方／ repair

Activities

How to Begin

〈 For pairs or groups 〉

息子：うわぁ、どこで ⋯⋯ を見つけたの？
Son: Wow! Where did you find …?

〈 For individuals 〉

昔は、
In olden days,

Activity Notes

骨董品 / an antique
リモコンで操作する / operate by remote control
（面倒だから）〜したくない / can't be bothered
白黒 / monochrome
シンプルな機能 / simple functions
使いやすい / easy to use
つまみをひねる / turn a knob

関連ユニット： Unit 6

Activities

Unit 5 Composition

Activity 8　ショッピングモールにて / At a Shopping Mall

あなたは新しいショッピングモールへ遊びに来た建築学科の学生です。
上図を参考に感想を述べてみましょう。

You are an architecture student travelling to a new shopping mall. Referring to the above diagram, describe your impression of the mall.

Activities

How to Begin
このショッピングモールは ……
This shopping mall is …

Activity Notes
ゾーンに分けて配置される / be divided into several zones
配置 / placement
メリハリ / accent, contrast
構成 / constitution, composition
リズム感がある / have a certain rhythm
基本モジュールで構成されている / be based on a basic module

関連ユニット：Unit 8

Activities

Unit 6　Sense

Activity 9　対照的なイメージ / Image Contrast

周囲を見まわして、対照的なイメージを持つ服を着た二人を選んで、イメージの違いを話し合いましょう。

Choose two people from around you who are wearing contrasting clothing styles and discuss the differences between them.

1人で学習する人は、下の写真の例を見て二つの違いについて説明しましょう。

<u>Instructions for individual study:</u>

Look at the following pictures of people and practice describing the differences between them.

A

B

132

Activities

How to Begin

Aは……を着ていて……のように見えます。

I think person A is wearing a ... that makes the wearer appear ...

Activity Notes

Aに対してBは、……である。

A is ..., on the other hand, B is ...

In contrast to A, B is wearing ...

The clothing that A is wearing contrasts with B's clothing because ...

関連ユニット： Unit 1 Unit 2 Unit 3 Unit 5

Activities

Unit 6 Sense

Activity 10　好きな理由 / Reasons for Liking Something

身の周りのカタログに掲載されている商品から好きな色と嫌いな色を選び、その理由を説明しましょう。

Choose a product from a nearby or online shopping catalog and explain what you like and dislike about it concerning the colors.

1人で学習する人は下の写真を見て、好きな色とその理由を説明しましょう。

Instructions for individual study:

Look at the following pictures and practice describing them.

134

Activities

How to Begin

この(商品)の(色)が好きです。
I prefer (the color) of (product).

Activity Notes

好み / preference
〜の方を好む / prefer to ...
〜しそう（〜になりそう）/ be likely to ...
〜できそう / could be ...
相性が良い（補って完全にする）/ complement
全体的に / overall

関連ユニット： Unit 2 Unit 3 Unit 5 Unit 8

Activities

Unit 6 Sense

Activity 11   色のイメージ / Color Image

カタログに掲載されている商品のカラーバリエーションを見て、各色のイメージの違いについてパートナーに説明し、意見交換をしましょう。

Choose a product line-up from a nearby or online catalog, and explain how the different colors express the image of each product. Exchange opinions with a partner.

1人で学習する人は、下の写真のカラーバリエーションを見て、各色のイメージの違いについて説明し、解答例と比較しましょう。

<u>*Instructions for individual study:*</u>
Compare your description of the picture below with the sample answer.

Activities

How to Begin

この（商品）の（色）は……。
The (color) of this (product) would look …

Activity Notes

〜に似合いそう / would look good on …
〜（のように）みえる / look …
人目を引く / eye-catching

関連ユニット： Unit 1　Unit 3　Unit 5　Unit 8

Activities

Unit 6 Sense

Activity 12   建築物の印象 / Architecture Impression

建築物の写真（美術館、橋、門）を比較し、その建築から受けるイメージの違いを説明してみましょう。

Compare the architecture in the pictures and explain their similarities and differences.

1人で学習する人は、下の写真を見て2つの建物のイメージの違いを説明し、解答例と比較してみましょう。

Instructions for individual study:
Looking at the pictures below, describe the architectural differences. Compare your description with the sample answer.

How to Begin

AとBは……に関する2つの例です。
A and B are two examples of ...

Guggenheim Museum N.Y.

The Museum of Modern Art

138

Activities

Activity Notes

グッゲンハイム美術館ニューヨーク / Guggenheim Museum N.Y.
MoMA（ニューヨーク近代美術館）/ The Museum of Modern Art
オルセー美術館 / Musée d'Orsay
ポンピドゥー・センター / Centre Pompidou
ミレニアム・ブリッジ / London Millennium Footbridge
ポンテ・ヴェッキオ / Ponte Vecchio
ノートルダム・デュ・オー / Chapelle Notre-Dame du Haut
ラ・トゥーレット修道院 / Couvent de la Tourette

現代でも / even today
増築 / extension
内側（室内）の / interior
印象 / impression
〜の印象を与える / appear ...
クラシカルな / classical
ハイテクな / high technological
有機的な / organic
幾何学的な / geometric
荒々しい / rugged
吊り橋 / suspension bridge
回遊式 / circuit-style
通り抜け / thorough

Musée d'Orsay

Centre Pompidou

London Millennium Footbridge

Ponte Vecchio

Chapelle Notre-Dame du Haut

Couvent de la Tourette

関連ユニット： Unit 1 Unit 2 Unit 3 Unit 5 Unit 8 Unit 9 Unit 10

139

Activities

Unit 7　Scale

Activity 13　図面のスケール / The Scale of Drawings

下の文章に Activity Notes に示す中から適切な縮尺を選んで入れましょう。
Choose the correct scale from the Activity Notes.

1) ヘアドライヤーのような、人が手に持てるプロダクトを描く場合は、図面の縮尺を＜ a ＞で描くのが一般的です。
   When drawing something that a person can hold in their hand, such as a hair dryer, normally you draw on a scale of ＜ a ＞.

2) 時計のような、小さくてディテールが細かいものは、＜ b ＞の縮尺で描きます。
   Things that are small and made with great detail, such as wristwatches, are drawn on a scale of ＜ b ＞.

3) 車のモデルは＜ c ＞や＜ d ＞の縮尺で作られます。
   A model of a car is made on a scale of ＜ c ＞ or ＜ d ＞.

4) 図面の CAD データは、＜ e ＞の縮尺で入力します。
   When drawing with CAD, one should enter the figures on a scale of ＜ e ＞.

5) 建築の平面図で住宅などの場合、縮尺は＜ f ＞が一般的です。
   In an architectural floor plan for houses, the dimensions are shown on a scale of ＜ f ＞.

6) 建築の図面でも、都市計画との関係を考えるには＜ g ＞の縮尺で描くだろう。
   In architectural drawings related to city planning, one may draw on a scale of ＜ g ＞.

7) 縮尺＜ h ＞の図面で 5 cm のものは、実際の大きさでは 10cm です。
   5cm on a ＜ h ＞ drawing is 10cm in actual size.

Activities

Activity Notes

1/1000 (one thousandth) / 1:1000 (one to one thousand)

1/200 (one two-hundredth) / 1:200 (one to two hundred)

1/100 (one hundredth) / 1:100 (one to one hundred)

1/10 (one tenth) / 1:10 (one to ten)

1/5 (one fifth) / 1:5 (one to five)

1/2 (one half) / 1:2 (one to two)

1/1 (same scale) / 1:1 (one to one)

2/1 (two times) / 2:1 (double scale)

Activities

Unit 8　Situation

Activity 14　ターゲットと使用シーン / Target and Scene

身の周りの商品デザインあるいは住宅デザインに対して、想定されるターゲットと使用シーンについて話し合いましょう。また、使用にあたっての問題点を挙げてみましょう。

Choose a nearby product or house design and discuss it in terms of its likely target users and how it is used. Make sure to consider any problems that might occur when using the product.

1人で学習する人は、下の製品について自分の説明と解答例を比較してみましょう。
Instructions for individual study:
Compare your explanations with the sample answer.

（例）商品：	POPカラーのポータブルスピーカー
(e.g.) product:	POP Color Portable Speaker
1. ターゲット：	＜流行に敏感な＞女子学生
Target user:	Students from ages 10 - 20, especially young girls who are sensitive to popular trends.
2. 使用シーン：	放課後、友達とダンスの練習のために、屋外で
Scene:	After school, some friends gather outside of a room to dance
3. 問題点：	ターゲット層の狭さによる＜少ない販売台数＞、＜すぐに流行遅れになる＞など
Practical issues:	The target users are too few, limiting sales. Products like this go out of style quickly.

Activities

How to Begin

〈 For pairs or groups 〉

この商品の想定されるターゲットは誰ですか？

Who is the target user for this product?

この商品はどのような場面で使われると思いますか？

In what setting do you think this product would be used?

〈 For individuals 〉

この商品の主なターゲットは …… だと思います。

I think the main target user of this product is ...

Activity Notes

どんな場面で / in what setting

問題点 / problems, the negative points

音質 / sound quality

コスト / cost

設置場所 / setting space

危険性 / danger

流行おくれ / out of style

ニッチな / niche

関連ユニット： Unit 1 Unit 2 Unit 3 Unit 4 Unit 5 Unit 6 Unit 9 Unit 10

143

Activities

Unit 8　Situation

Activity 15　どのネクタイが好き？ / Which Ties Do You Like?

デパートのネクタイ売り場で、店員と客が話しています。2人の会話を想像して、ロールプレイングをしてみましょう。

In the tie section of a department store, a customer talks with a salesperson. Make a dialogue between the customer and salesperson. Role-play the scenario with a partner.

1人で学習する人は、上の条件をもとに会話を想定して、解答例と比較してみましょう。

Instructions for individual study:
Make a dialogue between the customer and salesperson that includes the above information. Compare your dialogue with the sample dialogue.

Activities

How to Begin

店員：……だと思います。
Salesperson: I think that …

Activity Notes

店員 / salesperson
似合う / match
しっくり来ない / do not do it for me
〜の柄 / ... pattern
お買得 / on sale
客 / customer
つまらない / too plain
面白い / interesting

関連ユニット：Unit 1　Unit 2　Unit 3　Unit 6

Activities

Unit 8　Situation

Activity 16　建築家とクライアント / Client & Architect

下の条件に従って、クライアントと建築家の間で交わされる会話を想定し、ロールプレイングをしましょう。
Make a dialogue between a client and an architect that includes the information below. Role-play the scenario with a partner.

- クライアントが家を建てるために2つの敷地候補を建築家と相談しています。
  A client is consulting with an architect about building a house on one of two different sites.
- クライアントは各敷地の特徴を説明し、建築家はそこに建つ家を提案します。
  The client is explaining the different characteristics of each site and the architect is offering building suggestions.
- クライアントの奥さんは演劇が好きで、都市部に住みたがっています。
  The client's wife enjoys going to the theater and prefers to live in the city.

- 敷地1：山の中腹。海を見下ろし、見晴らしがいい。駅からのアクセスが悪い。
  In the mountains, with a view of the sea. The view is good but access to the train station is poor.
- 敷地2：駅に近く、都市部にある。かつては劇場が建っていた。
  Close to the station, in an urban area. It used to be the site of a theater.

1人で学習する人は、先の条件をもとに会話を想定し解答例と比較してみましょう。
Instructions for individual study:
Make a dialogue between the client and the architect that includes the above information. Compare your dialogue with the sample dialogue.

Activities

How to Begin

クライアント：この敷地は……
Client: The site …

Activity Notes

リラックスできる家 / a house you can relax in
〜のような家 / a house like …
〜の場所に住む / live in a place …

敷地 1

敷地 2

関連ユニット： Unit 6

147

Activities

Unit 9　Light and Shadow

Activity 17　目覚まし時計の表示 / Alarm Clock Display

目覚まし時計の表示について、設問に対するアイデアを出しあってみましょう。
Think about a new kind of display for an alarm clock. Consider the following in your design.

- 暗闇でも時間がわかるようにするためには？
  How can you tell the time in the dark?
- 明るい場所でも見やすくするためには？（液晶表示の場合）
  How will you make it easy to read? (for an LCD)
- 光を使ってユニバーサルデザインへの配慮ができるか？
  How can the illumination be used in terms of universal design?

1人で学習する人は、上の設問に対するアイデアを解答例と比較してみましょう。
Instructions for individual study:
Compare your description with the sample answers.

Activities

How to Begin

〈 For pairs or groups 〉

暗闇でも時間がわかるような目覚まし時計の表示に対するアイデアはないかな？

Do you have any ideas for an alarm clock display that will tell the time in the dark?

〈 For individuals 〉

〜するためには……

In order to ...

Activity Notes

液晶画面 / LCD screen

バックライト / backlight

蓄光塗料 / light storage coating material

フラッシュ / flash

だんだん明るくなる / gradually brighten

照らす / illuminate

聴覚または視覚に障害のある / hearing or vision impaired

調整 / adjusting

関連ユニット：Unit 1 Unit 3 Unit 6 Unit 8 Unit 10

Activities

Unit 9　Light and Shadow

Activity 18　暮らしと照明 / Lifestyle and Lighting

住宅では各部屋においてさまざまな照明効果が必要です。リビングやダイニングなどそれぞれの場所に適した照明について、その種類や明るさ、形、素材について、パートナーと話し合ってみましょう。

Every room in a home requires a different kind of lighting effect. Discuss with your partner about the appropriate type, brightness, form and materials for a living room, dining room and other rooms.

1人で学習する人は下の条件をもとに各部屋に合う照明を考え、解答例と比較してみましょう。

Instructions for individual study:

Describe the appropriate lighting conditions for the rooms listed below, and compare your description with the sample answer.

- ダイニング ― 部屋全体を明るくしたい。

    Dining room ― illuminate the entire room
- キッチン ― 調理する素材の色を確認したい。

    Kitchen ― easy to see the color and condition of the food
- リビング ― エレガントな雰囲気にしたい。

    Living room ― elegant atmosphere

How to Begin

〈 For pairs or groups 〉

……にはどんな種類の照明を選びますか？

What kind of lighting would you choose for ...?

〈 For individuals 〉

私は部屋全体を明るくするための……がよいと思います。

I think ... to illuminate the entire room would be good.

Activities

Activity Notes

場所
浴室 / bath　　トイレ / restroom　　門 / gate　　寝室 / bedroom　　キッチン / kitchen

位置
ブラケット / wall light
シーリングライト / ceiling light
卓上スタンド / desk light
足元灯 / foot light

種類
シャンデリア / chandelier
ペンダントライト / pendant light
間接照明 / indirect light

その他
昼光色 / fluorescent
電球色 / incandescent
内蔵する / built-in
目立たない / nondescript
安らぐ / soothing, comforting
演出する / direct
読める / readable
調光機能 / lighting adjustment function
〜（素材）を使った / made from ..., made with ...
A をモチーフにした B 調のデザイン / B style design using (material) with A motif

関連ユニット：Unit 1　Unit 3　Unit 6　Unit 8　Unit 10

Activities

Unit 10　Function

Activity 19　各種製品と機能 / Product Function

常識を打ち破るような夢の家電製品の機能について、アイデアを出し合ってみましょう。次に、そのアイデアについて、問題点や配慮すべき点を話し合ってみましょう。

Talk about some ideas for revolutionary new functions of home appliances. After you have decided on your new functions, discuss the possible problems and safety considerations.

1人で学習する人は、下の例に挙げられた製品において想定される問題点や安全性について説明し、解答例と比較してみましょう。

Instructions for individual study:

Describe the possible problems and safety considerations for the product listed below and compare your explanation with the sample answer.

（例）「乗って動き回ることができる楽しい掃除機」

(e.g.) a fun vacuum cleaner that you can ride on.

Activities

How to Begin

〈 For class 〉

…… について、何か面白いアイデアはあるかな？

Do you have any good ideas on/for …?

〈 For individuals 〉

私達がその製品をデザインするにあたって配慮すべき問題は ……

In order to design that product, we need to consider the following problems;

Activity Notes

新規性 / new feature

自ら洗浄する製品 / self-cleaning product

手で持つ（もの）/ handheld

固定して / in a fixed space

移動して使う / use while moving

引き回す / drag around

使用後の片づけ / clean-up after use

安全性への配慮 / safety considerations

存在感 / presence

関連ユニット： Unit 1 Unit 2 Unit 3 Unit 4
　　　　　　　 Unit 5 Unit 6 Unit 8 Unit 9

Activities

Unit 11　Application

Activity 20　コンペティションへの応募 / Application for a Competition

コンペティションへの応募用紙を書いてみましょう。下の書類規定に従ってください。

Fill in an application sheet for a competition. Follow the text and document formatting rules.

DREAM CG Art Award

Theme: Can be about anything. Still picture to be expressed in CG. "DREAM CG Art Award" calls for excellence in CG arts, being unique and having visual attraction that goes beyond the conventional standpoint of existing art or movie industry.

General Rules

- Must be an original CG work created in 2014 or later.
- Any corporations, either individual or groups are all welcome, regardless of age, sex, professional background, or nationality.
- Applicant can apply for more than one category.
- Applicant is responsible for receiving proper permission when using the work of an outside party (art, movie, photograph or music) as materials in the submission.
- One applicant can submit up to two works.

Application Period: May 20 - August 20, 2015.

Privileges for the Winners: Winning works will be exhibited at DREAM Gallery for 10 days.

Activities

Entry Fees: Free of charge

How to Submit: Push the "Registration" button on the Application website and proceed with the application that follows the guide.

Prepare Your Work and Documents According to the Following Guidelines:
Captured image size of the work; the width should be within the range of 480 to 640 pixels, but the height is not specified. For any work with a height or width larger than 640 pixels, the file will be automatically compressed.

File Format: JPEG(RGB), PNG, GIF

Mail address: Indicate an e-mail address where you can be contacted.

Presentation Sheet: Title, Concept (Within 200 words), Creator's name or group name, Creator's biography (Within 100 words)

※ By applying for the DREAM CG Art Award, the applicant agrees to all of the provisions of the application process.

関連ユニット: Unit 1 Unit 2 Unit 3 Unit 4 Unit 5
Unit 6 Unit 7 Unit 8 Unit 9 Unit 10

Activities

Presentation Sheet for Initial Judging

1. Title

2. Concept (Within 200 words)

3. Creator's name or group name

4. Creator's biography (Within 100 words)

Activity Guide

Activity Guide
Color

性質の表現

● 明るい色使い	bright	I would like to express a clean product image by using bright colors. (明るい色使いで製品のクリーンなイメージを表現したい)
	brilliant	The brilliant city lights are very beautiful. (キラキラした街の明かりが美しい)
	dazzling	The Christmas ornaments are dazzling under the bright lights. (クリスマスのオーナメントが照明にあたってキラキラしている)
● 暗い色使い	dark, bleak	I would like to express the sadness of the character by using dark colors. (暗い色使いで登場人物の悲しみを表現したい)
● ヴィヴィッドな	vivid	We would like to get people's attention by using vivid colors for the bags. (ヴィヴィッドな色をバッグに使って注目を集めたい)
● シックな	chic	Use chic colors to give a calm impression. (シックな色遣いで落ち着いた印象を与えなさい)
● 背景色	background color	Sky blue is often used for the background color of car rendering. (スカイブルーは車のレンダリングの背景色によく使われる)
● 無彩色	absence of color	Don't you think the absence of color leaves a dreary impression? (無彩色だと寒々しく感じるね)
● 明度差	brightness gap	If you don't have a larger brightness gap between the background color and the letters, it will be difficult to read. (地色と文字の明度差をもっとつけないと読めないよ)
● 彩度の高い色	highly saturated colors	Use highly saturated colors. (彩度の高い色を使いなさい)
● 明度の高い	light, high level of lightness	Since the background color is dark, let's use a lighter color for the letters. (背景色が暗いから、文字色はもっと明度の高い色を使おう)
● 暖色系の色	warm colors	There is a tendency to use warm colors for heating appliances. (暖房器具には暖色系の色を多用する傾向がある)
● クール系の色	cool colors	Let's use cool colors for the shaved ice machine. (かき氷機にはクール系の色を使おう)

Activity Guide
Color

●	フリップフロップ（色変化が大きいさま）	flipflopping	Flipflopping is a term used to describe how the color changes according to the angle of sight. （フリップフロップとは、1つの色が見る角度によって異なって見える現象である）
●	ハイライトとシェード	highlight and shade	This color alternates depending on the highlights and shade. （この色はハイライトとシェードの部分の見え方が変わる）
●	抑制の効いた色使い	conservative use of the colors	Conservative use of the colors leaves an impact and adds elegance. （抑制の効いた色使いがインパクトがありながらも上品な感じに仕上げている）

行為・効果

●	～(色)で目立たせる	use ... colors to make (it) stand out	Use complimentary colors like red and green to make the composition stand out. （赤や緑などの補色を使うことで構成を目立たせなさい）
●	色の統一感を出す	unify the colors	I want to unify the colors using the same hue. （同系色で統一感を出したい）
●	～となじむ	blend in with	The color of the wall is good, because it blends in with the surrounding area. （この壁の色は周りの環境になじんでいていいね）
●	同じ色調でなじませる	blend in with the colors of the same color tone	Blend the dark red in other with the colors of the same color tone. （その暗い赤を他と同じ色調でなじませてください）
●	～を暗くする	darken	Since the lime green is too bright, why don't we darken the color to give a calm impression? （このライムグリーンが明るすぎるので、暗くして落ち着いた感じにしてはどうかな）
●	～を明るくする	lighten, brighten	Let's lighten the color to give it a happier feel. （色を明るくしてハッピーな感じにしよう）
●	まとめる	bring together	Let's use orange for the letters in this area to bring it all together. （このエリアの文字はすべてオレンジ系でまとめよう）

Activity Guide
Color

● バランスをとる	add balance, use ... for consistency（一貫性）	This area is too bright. I think you should add balance by using dark colors. （ここは明るすぎるね。暗い色を使ってバランスをとった方がいい）	
● ハレーション	halation, spreading out of light, radiance, aura	Halation occurs when the contrast between opposite colors is strengthened. （ハレーションは補色を用いてコントラストを強めたときに起きる）	
● 注意を引く	draw attention, call attention, get attention	Warning signs should use colors that draw people's attention. （警告サインは注意を引く色がいい）	
● だんだん明るくする	gradually lighten	Gradually lighten from the bottom to the top. （下から徐々に明るくしなさい）	
● 色味を足す	add a little shade	Make it more cheerful by adding a little shade. （色味を足してもっと元気な感じにしよう）	
● グラデーション	gradation, gradual change of color	Gradation is a gradual change of color. （グラデーションとは少しずつ色が変化することだ）	
● 差し色を効かせる	use an accent color	Since the overall impression is vague, let's use an accent color to sharpen the image. （全体の印象がぼやっとしているから、差し色を効かせて引き締めよう）	
● 黒い〜で強調する	The black ... emphasize	The black outline emphasizes the pink area. （黒い縁取りでピンクの部分を強調する）	
● 〜を引き締める	sharpen, tighten	Since the overall impression is vague, let's add a small highlight to sharpen the image. （全体の印象がぼやっとしているから、少しハイライトを入れて引き締めよう）	
● 〜にアクセントをつける	accentuate, emphasize	Insert a small, bright red dot to accentuate the pattern. （パターンにアクセントをつけるために小くて鮮やかな赤い点を入れなさい）	
● コントラストをつける	add contrast	It is better to add contrast between A and B. （AとBのコントラストをつけた方がいい）	
● 〜に軽さを出す	lighten	Let's use bright colors to lighten it up. （明るい色を使って軽さを出そう）	
● 二色で印刷する	print in two colors	Print in two colors to save costs. （二色刷りにしてコストを抑えなさい）	

Activity Guide
Color

● ～を加飾する	decorate	The exterior is too simple, so let's decorate it a little. （外観がシンプルすぎるので、少し加飾しよう）

イメージ表現

● ～らしい色	…ish, …like, …-friendly	
子どもらしい色	childlike/child-friendly colors	Let's use childlike colors for toys. （おもちゃには子どもらしい色を使おう）
南国らしい色	tropical colors	Let's use tropical colors for floats. （浮き輪には南国らしい色を使おう）
京都らしい色	a color that is reminiscent of Kyoto, Kyoto colors	Let's use a color that is reminiscent of Kyoto. （京都らしい色を使おう）
● ～を彷彿させる（色）	the (color) reminds people of	That purple reminds people of Kyoto. （紫色は京都を彷彿させる）
● ～によく合う	good for, fit (match), suit	These colors are good for Kyoto. （この色は京都によく合う）
● ～風の	… style	I wonder which color composition is more appropriate; Japanese, western, or Asian style. （和風か洋風かアジア風か、どの配色が良いか悩むね）
● 重厚感のある色	deep color	I think we should use deep colors for this car. （この車には重厚感のある色を使うべきだ）
● 抜けが良い	clear, light	It is too heavy like this. We need more clear colors that lighten the mood a little. （このままだと重い感じだから、雰囲気を明るくする抜けの良い色を使いたい）
● ソリッドライク	a feeling of solidity, solidness	This color gives a feeling of solidity, and it has a good metallic effect that adds depth to the image. （この色はソリッドライクだけど、メタリックのエフェクトがうまく出て深みがある）

Activity Guide
Color

● ギラギラ感（派手な感じ）のある	gaudy, glaring, glittering	This car is targeted at wild people, so let's add more gaudy metallic colors. （この車のターゲットはちょっとワルい人達だから、メタリックを多めに入れたギラギラ感のある色を加えよう）
● 古臭い	outdated	Don't you think this color balance is outdated? （この配色、古臭くないかな）
● 若々しい配色	vibrant/youthful/ energetic/young style/fresh/lively colors	This hair dryer is targeted at people fresh out of college, so let's use vibrant colors. （このドライヤーは新社会人がターゲットだから、若々しい色で塗ろう）
● 自然な色使い	natural colors	This picture is well balanced with natural colors. （この絵は自然な色とよく調和する）
● 素材を活かした	use the materials effectively	This composition uses the materials effectively. （素材を有効に使った構成だ）
● ほんのりした	soft, pale, slightly	I like the soft pink used for Japanese sweets. （和菓子に使われているほんのりしたピンクが好きだ）
● 生成りの	unbleached	Let's make it look natural by using unbleached cloth. （生成りの布でナチュラル感を演出しよう）
● ニュアンスがある	have a subtle nuance	The soft purple has a subtle nuance of nobility. （淡い紫色は高貴なニュアンスがある）

その他

● 色溜まり（色が濃く深く見えること）	color looks deeper and darker	The color looks deeper and darker at the bottom, making the car body appear heavy. （下の部分の色溜まりがボディーを重く見せる）
● ベーシックカラー	basic colors	Let's only provide the basic colors, white, black and silver for this car. （この車は白と黒とシルバーのベーシックカラーのみで展開しよう）
● 材料着色	colored materials, material coloring	Let's use colored materials for the parts of the switch. （スイッチのパーツは材料着色を使おう）

Activity Guide
Color

● 着色顔料	colored pigment	The new color uses pigment effectively. This color brings out the best of colored pigment. (新色は顔料を効果的に使っている。着色顔料の効果を最大限に引き出した色だ)	
● 彩度	saturation	Saturation is a measurement of how different from pure grey the color is. (彩度は無彩色からの差異を測る尺度である)	
● 明度	lightness, value, luminosity	Lightness is the scale of tone from light to dark. (明度は明るい色から暗い色への尺度である)	
● 発色	intensity, brilliance, vividness	The high color intensity is not so effective at night. (夜は発色の高い色がその効果を発揮できない)	
● 色相(色味・色調)	chroma, hue	Chroma refers to the intensity of color. (色相とは色あいのことだ)	
● 補色	complementary color	Use complementary colors to add impact. (補色を使ってインパクトを与えなさい)	
● 同系色	same color tone	I want to use the same color tone to give wholeness. (同系色でまとまり感を出したい)	
● 色使い	use of colors	The use of bright colors would give a vibrant image. (明るい色使いで元気なイメージにする)	
● 配色	color arrangement	You should consider the color arrangement before painting. (塗る前に配色をよく考えるべきだ)	
● 配色がよい	color arrangement is good	The color arrangement of this composition is especially good. (この構成は特に配色がいい)	
● 色覚	color perception	Eye color can affect color perception. (目の色で色覚も変わるらしい)	
● 色彩計画	color scheme	He planned the color scheme of this town. (彼がこの街の色彩計画を立てた)	

Activity Guide
Form

形状の表現 （具象的／抽象的）

具象的

●	ゲート状の	gate-like	There is a gate-like monument in the central area. （中央にゲート状のモニュメントがある）
●	シャープなハイライトエッジ	sharp highlighted edge	I would like to bring out the sharp highlighted edges as much as possible. （できるだけシャープなハイライトエッジを見せたい）
●	ハイライトを通す	highlights come out, highlight straight	The highlights on the car shoulder line did not come out smoothly. （ショルダーのハイライトがキレイに通っていない）
●	握りやすい形	shape that is easy to hold	Let's design a handle in a shape that is easy to hold. （ハンドルは握りやすい形状にデザインしよう）
●	スリットを入れる	put in/add a slit	Put in a slit to act as the intake port. （吸気口としてスリットを入れなさい）
●	スリット	slit	A cool breeze blows from a slit in the ceiling. （天井のスリット部分から冷風が出る）
●	テーパーのついた	tapered	The shape should be tapered. （テーパーのついた形にするべきだ）
●	テーパーをつける	add a taper, make ... tapered	Adding a taper improves the drainage capacity. （テーパーをつけることで水はけを良くする）
●	きつい角度のテーパー	hard taper	The hard taper makes it slippery. （テーパーがきついため滑り落ちてしまう）
●	テーパー角度	angle of the taper	I think we should give more consideration to the angle of the taper. （もっとテーパー角度を考慮するべきだ）
●	抜きテーパーの無い	without a decreasing taper	I really want to finish this without a decreasing taper. （抜きテーパーの無い状態で仕上げたい）
●	下に行くほど細くなる	narrow as it goes down	The shape narrows as it goes down, which adds an airy quality to it. （下に行くほど細くなる形で軽さを表現する）

Activity Guide

Form

●	徐々に広がる	open up gradually	The mouth opens up gradually as the opening gets larger. (口が徐々に広がって開口部が大きくなる)
●	アールをつける	round the corners	Let's round the corners. (角にアールをつけよう)
●	アールを大きくする	increase the radius	By increasing the radius, we can make the tear disappear. (アールを大きくするとキレが無くなる)
●	アールを徐変すること	gradually changing radius	A gradually changing radius decreases the chances of error. (アールを徐変させることでごまかすしかない)
●	切り込み	notch	There are notches on the surface to hold onto. (面に切れ込みを入れ引っかかりをつくる)
●	AからBへの緩やかな変化	gradual change from A to B	There is a gradual change from a curved to a flat surface. (曲面から平面への緩やかな変化がある)
●	右に下がる	droop downward on the right	The sign looks good, but the logo droops downward on the right. (このロゴは良いと思うけど、右下がりに見えるね)
●	傾斜した	sloping	The downward sloping floor makes effective use of the space. (傾斜した床がスペースをうまく使っている)
●	傾斜をつける	increase the slope	Increase the slope of the roof. (屋根に傾斜をつけなさい)
●	○分の1の勾配	incline/angle of ○ %	For drainage, we added a 1/50 incline to the flooring. (水はけのため、床に50分の1の勾配をつける)
●	片流れの	one-sided	One-sided roofs look daring. (片流れの屋根は大胆に見える)
●	〜より○cm高い	○ cm higher than ...	The floor is set to be 20cm higher than ground level. (床面はグランドレベルより20cm高い)
●	〜より○cm低い	○ cm lower than ...	The floor is set to be 20cm lower than ground level. (床面はグランドレベルより20cm低い)
●	流線形の	streamlined	The streamlined shape gives the feeling of speed. (流線型を用いてスピード感を出す)
●	とがった形の	pointed, sharp	There are offices in that pointed building over there. (あのとがった形のビルにオフィスがある)
●	らせん状の	spiral	The double spiral staircase leads upstairs. (二重らせん状の階段が上に導いている)

Activity Guide
Form

● ロの字型の	square-shaped	The overview shows a square-shaped structure. （プランビューで見るとロの字型の建屋となっている）	
● コの字型の	U-shaped	The site of the schoolhouse is U-shaped. （コの字型の校舎が建っている）	
● 塔状の	tower-like	The tower-like structure has a clock on it. （塔状の部分に時計がある）	
● 薄く鋭い	thin and sharp	The tip is thin and sharp. （先端部は薄く鋭い形状となっている）	
● 深く細長い	long, thin, deep	The long, thin, deep ditches run parallel. （深く細長い溝が何本も平行に走っている）	
● 浅く広い	wide/big and shallow	There is a wide and shallow pond in the front. （前面に浅く広い池が配置されている）	
● 奥深い	deep	The stair goes deep underground. （奥深い地下へと階段が続いている）	
● （間口に対して）奥行の深い	narrow but deep	The frontage of old homes in Kyoto were narrow but deep. （昔ながらの京都の家は、間口に対して奥行が深い）	
● 奥行の浅い	shallow depth	A characteristic of this counter is its shallow depth. （奥行の浅いカウンターを特徴とする）	
● ボクシーな	boxy	The boxy shape allows for better luggage storage capacity. （ボクシーな形状で荷物が沢山積める）	
● 格子模様	checkered pattern	The checkered pattern on the window makes it feel Japanese. （窓の格子模様が和風の味を出している）	
● 水玉模様	polka dots	She is famous for her art that contains many polka dots. （彼女は水玉模様で有名なアーティストだ）	
● 縞模様	stripes	If I look at it slantwise, it seems like the stripes are floating. （斜めから見ると縞模様が浮き出る）	
● リブ形状	ribbed shape	By using a ribbed shape, it's possible to keep it both lightweight and strong. （リブ形状を採用することで、軽量化と強度の両立をはかることができる）	
● 幾何学的な	geometric, geometrical, formal	He likes to use geometric patterns for the garden. （彼は庭に幾何学的なパターンを使用することを好む）	

166

Activity Guide
Form

抽象的

● 自由な曲線の	natural/free curve	Recently the use of natural curves in architecture has increased. （最近は自由な曲線の建築が増えた）
● 直線的な	linear	The linear silhouette makes this car look fast. （直線的なシルエットで速そうな車だ）
● どこにも直線が無い	nothing is linear	In the natural world, nothing is linear. （自然界にはどこにも直線が無い）
● 動的な形	dynamic/kinetic shape	I would like to use dynamic shapes as symbols in the monument. （シンボルとして動的な形のモニュメントにしたい）
● 静的な形	static form	Using a static form for the shape projects a calm feeling. （静的な形が落ち着きをもたらす）
● ダイナミックな	dynamic	The dynamic shape looks powerful. （ダイナミックな形状で勢いを感じる）
● でこぼこした	uneven, rough	I traveled along the uneven surface of the cobblestone streets. （石畳のでこぼこした路面を走行した）
● でこぼこ	ridges	I put ridges on the handle to make it easy to hold. （持ちやすいようにハンドルにでこぼこを付けた）
● 壮大な	grand, imposing	The view of the grand vista was moving. （壮大な景色に感動した）
● ごつごつした	rugged	The rugged shape gives the impression of manliness. （ごつごつした形で男性的な印象を与える）
● ふくらみをつける	round out	Round out the surface so that it doesn't look dented. （引けて見えないようにふくらみをつけなさい）
● くぼみをつける	add a cavity	Add a cavity to make it look like it is full of water. （水でいっぱいに見えるように、くぼみをつけなさい）
● ボリューム感のある形	voluminous shape	The voluminous shape makes it appear larger than it really is. （ボリューム感のある形にして実物よりも大きく見せる）
● 優美な曲線	elegant/graceful curve	The elegant curves give the product a high-quality appearance. （優美な曲線が製品の高級感を出している）
● 緩やかな曲線	gentle curve	The gentle curves of the rooftop wind smoothly. （屋根が緩やかな曲線で滑らかにうねっている）

Activity Guide
Form

● 滑らかなうねり	smooth undulation	The smooth undulations are a characteristic feature of the winding rooftop. （滑らかなうねりがこの屋根を特徴づけている）
● 先進的な	cutting-edge	Bold use of curved lines resulted in the construction of a cutting-edge building. （曲線を大胆に使った先進的な建築物だ）
● チリを合わせる	even out the spaces	Evening out the spaces between the shapes improves the quality. （チリを合わせることで質感が向上する）
● 隙（クリアランス）を取る	fill in the gap	If we don't fill in the gaps, they might become a bigger problem later. （隙を取らないと、後で大きな問題となる）
● 面一にする（つらを合わせる）	make the surface flush	Making the surfaces flush together is a recent trend. （面一にすることが最近のトレンドだ）
● ～に段ちをつける	make ... uneven	Making it uneven on purpose accentuates this part of the product. （わざと段ちをつけて部品を強調する）
● ～を絞る	squeeze	Squeezing the back part will make it more aerodynamic. （後ろの部分を絞ることでもっと空力が良くなる）
● メカニカルな	mechanical	The mechanical movements are interesting. （メカニカルな動きが面白い）
● 折れ感	fold	We need to highlight the folds in the car body. （車のボディーにもっと折れ感を出す必要がある）

イメージ表現

● 柔軟な	flexible	We should consider the possibility of being more flexible in order to meet customer demand. （顧客の要望によって柔軟な対応を考えるべきだ）
● ずんぐりとした	stocky	The stocky shape brings with it a sense of familiarity. （ずんぐりとした形で親近感を持たせる）
● 悪そうな	bad, seeming evil	This car has a "bad boy" image that has a certain charm. （この車は悪そうな顔立ちが魅力的だ）

Activity Guide
Form

● スムーズな	smooth	Can you make it smooth front to side? （フロントからサイドへスムーズな流れにできないかな）
● うるさい（要素が多い）	busy (with many elements)	It is too busy like this, so let's try for a more straightforward shape. （要素が多くてうるさいから、もっとスッキリした形にしよう）
● 精悍な	determined, fearless	He had a determined look on his face. （彼は精悍な顔をしていた）
● スッキリとした	straightforward	It is too busy like this, so let's try for a more straightforward shape. （要素が多くてうるさいから、もっとスッキリした形にしよう）
● ゴリっとした	uneven, rocky, rugged	The uneven shape, like a rocky surface, makes it look strong. （岩の表面のようなゴリっとした形が強そうに見える）
● ゴツい	rough, tough	I want a shape that makes it appear rough and tough. （もっとゴツいタフそうな形にしたい）
● 品のない	shoddy, graceless, unrefined	Your disorganized approach resulted in a shoddy design. （ごちゃごちゃしてて品の無いデザインだ）

〜感

● 圧迫感	an overpowering feeling	There is an overpowering feeling in the room. （室内に圧迫感がある）
● 精緻感	careful attention to the smallest detail	Measured down to the nearest millimeter, this shape was made with careful attention to the smallest detail. （ミリ単位の検討で、精緻感のある形に仕上がった）
● 安心感	a sense of security	It's important that people feel a sense of security when they sit in it. （中に座ったときの安心感が重要だ）
● 安定感	a sense of stability	It's important that people feel a sense of stability when they see it. （見た目の安定感が大切だ）
● 踏ん張り感	a sense of firmness	Having four wheels gives a sense of firmness. （タイヤが四隅にあって踏ん張り感がある）
● 塊感	solid	The body looks solid, giving it an overall strong impression. （本体の塊感が強く、存在感がある）

Activity Guide
Form

その他

- ● 機能的   practical, functional   This is a practical shape without any bells and whistles.
（無駄がない機能的な形だ）

- ● 端末（処理）   edge   You didn't think about the edge of the bumper.
（バンパーの端末処理が考えられていない）

- ● 辻褄が合わない   inconsistent   Continuing in this way is inconsistent with the shape of the design.
（このままでは形の辻褄が合わない）

- ● 面構成   surface layout   The surface layout is unrealistic and therefore it will be impossible to make.
（面構成に無理があって形が成立していない）

- ● 断面の強さ   cross-section strength   This car body has good cross-section strength.
（この車体には断面の強さがある）

- ● 〜らしい線使い   lines used in a ... style   These lines are used in an Italian style.
（イタリア人らしい線使いだ）

Activity Guide
Material

素材

● 鉄（板）	iron (plate)		The nature of iron's hardness can be changed based on heating and cooling. （鉄の硬度は加熱と冷却でさまざまに変化する）
● ステンレス	stainless steel		Stainless steel is rustproof, but the difficulty of the process is a drawback. （ステンレスは錆びには強いが、加工が難しいという欠点もある）
● チタン	titanium		Is there an advantage to using titanium alloys for making bicycles? （自転車作りにチタン合金を使う利点はありますか）
● マグネシウム	magnesium		Product designs that use magnesium require precise and advanced technology. （マグネシウムを使った製品設計は精密で高度な技術が必要だ）
● アルミダイキャスト	diecast aluminum		Using diecast aluminum would give a smoother finish. （アルミダイキャストにすることで滑らかな表面にできる）
● 錫	tin		Tin is often used as an alloy. （錫は合金として使われることが多い）
● 銅	copper		Copper has a warm feel to it and is also very workable. （銅は温かみを感じる色の金属で加工性も高い）
● プラスチック素材	plastic material		Since plastic material can be easily processed, it is utilized in various products and parts. （加工しやすいプラスチック素材はさまざまな製品や部品に活用されている）
● ポリカーボネート	polycarbonate		Polycarbonate is an example of a strong and transparent material. （ポリカーボネートは丈夫で透明感のある素材の一つだ）
● カーボン	carbon		Carbon is known for its lightness and strength. （カーボンは軽くて丈夫な素材として知られている）
● シリコン	silicon		Strong and flexible silicon material is one of the most versatile materials. （強度があり柔軟なシリコン素材は万能素材の一つだ）
● ABS 樹脂	ABS resin		ABS resin is the most common plastic material. （ABS 樹脂はもっとも一般的なプラスチック素材だ）

Activity Guide
Material

●	アクリル樹脂	acrylic resin	Acrylic resin, which is highly transparent, is rather expensive. (アクリル樹脂は透明度が高く、比較的高価な素材だ)
●	メラミン樹脂	melamine resin	Melamine resins are widely used in dishes. (メラミン樹脂は食器に多く使用されている)
●	発泡素材	foam material	By using flexible foam materials, various shapes and levels of hardness are possible. (弾力のある発泡素材を使用することにより、さまざまな形状や硬さが可能となる)
●	ウレタンフォーム	polyurethane foam	Polyurethane foam could be useful to provide thermal insulation. (ウレタンフォームは断熱素材として有効だ)
●	木材	wood	Wood with a sense of warmth is appropriate for the parts people hold and sit on. (握ったり座ったりする部分には温かみのある木材がふさわしい)
●	化粧板（単板）	veneer	Veneer is a suitable material to use for surfaces. (化粧板は表面材として適した素材だ)
●	無垢木	solid wood	Solid wood is widely used for exclusive furniture. (無垢の木材は高級な家具に多用されている)
●	集成材	laminated lumber/wood	You can reduce the cost of wooden products by using laminated lumber. (集成材を使うことで木製製品の価格を抑えることができる)
●	曲木	bentwood	Bentwood chairs look graceful. (曲木の椅子は優美である)
●	合板	plywood	Plywood is an indispensible material in modern industry. (合板は近代産業に欠かせない素材だ)
●	成型合板	molded plywood	Molded plywood is used in places such as chair seats and backrests. (椅子の座面や背もたれ等には、成型合板が使われている)
●	ブラスト加工	blast processing	Blast processing can result in a smoothness, giving a sense of luxury. (ブラスト加工による滑らかさにより高級感が出ている)
●	梨地（仕上げ）	satin (finish)	Satin (finish) gives an elegant and classy feel. (梨地仕上げは上品で高級感がある)
●	フロスト仕上げ	frost finish	Frost finish is suitable for the bathroom windows. (フロスト仕上げは浴室の窓にむいている)

Activity Guide
Material

●	ピアノフィニッシュ	piano finish	Piano finish adds a sense of luxury to products. (ピアノフィニッシュは製品に高級感を加える)
●	石目塗装	pebble finish	Pebble finish is a special technique that has become a necessary part of the coating process. (石目塗装は塗装過程で必要な特別なテクニックだ)
●	表面処理	surface treatment, finish	The texture of the material can be changed based on the surface treatment. (表面処理によって素材感が変化する)
●	再生材	recycled materials	It is possible to optimize the price by using recycled materials. (再生材を活用することで価格の適正化を図ることができる)
●	光輝材（光輝顔料）	glitter (material)	How about using glittering materials around the frame to add impact? (インパクトを与えるためにフレームに光輝材を使ってはどうかな)
●	隠ぺい性のある塗料	concealing paint	Use a concealing paint to cover the base. (隠ぺい性のある塗料で下地を隠しなさい)
●	遮へい材、シールド材	shielding material	The shielding material blocks electric waves from any other electronic products. (シールド材は電子製品の電波を遮断する)
●	緩衝材	buffer material	Buffer material protects the human body in a car accident. (緩衝材は自動車事故から人体を守る)
●	起毛調	brushed tone	The brushed-tone finish has improved the texture of the plastic. (起毛調仕上げのおかげでプラスチックの質感が向上している)
●	加工方法	processing method	Various processing methods have been tried out for different types of metal. (金属の種類によってさまざまな加工方法が工夫されてきた)
●	プレス加工	press (processing)	In general, press processing is widely used for car body. (一般的にプレス加工は車のボディーに多く使われている)
●	溶接	welding	Welding is an important process in the production line. (溶接は製造ラインにおいて重要な工程である)
●	メッキ加工	(galvanized) plating, galvanizing	Plating has improved the texture of products. (メッキは製品の質感を向上させてきた)
●	金属加工	metal working	Metal working has significantly contributed to the development of modern industry. (金属加工は近代産業を大きく発展させた)

Activity Guide
Material

● 折り曲げ加工	bending	Bending is one approach to increasing the strength of the plate. (折り曲げ加工は板材の強度を上げる手法の1つだ)
● 塗装仕上げ	painted surface finish	A painted surface finish gives the product a classy feel. (塗装仕上げによって高級感のある製品とする)

状況・状態

● 触感	touch, feel, sense	A good sense of touch is one of the most important features. (良い触感は大切な性能の一つだ)
● 硬い、硬質な	hard, solid	The surface of the table is hard, which protects it from damage. (そのテーブルの表面は硬く、傷がつきにくい)
● 硬度	hardness	This coating has a hardness that other coatings do not have. (この表面処理は他と比べて硬度が高い)
● 傷がつかない	scratch-proof	A good feature of this furniture is that it has a scratch-proof finish. (この家具は傷がつかない仕上げが特徴だ)
● 柔らかい	soft, gentle	Sofas with a soft touch sell well. (柔らかい肌触りのソファが良く売れる)
● 弾力性	elasticity, flexiblity	Material with elasticity can be used effectively to absorb shock and prevent slipping. (弾力性のある素材は衝撃吸収やすべり止めなどに効果があり、使われている)
● ふわふわした	fluffy	She has fluffy hair. (彼女の髪はふわふわしている)
● ぐらぐらする	wobble	I think there is a danger that it will wobble in a strong wind. (それは強風の中でぐらぐらすると思われます)
● 透明性、透過性	transparency	By utilizing materials with a sense of transparency it's possible to create a sense of cleanliness. (透明感のある素材を使うことで清潔感を出せる)
● 不透明な	opaque, nontransparent	Opaque material evokes a relaxed atmosphere. (不透明な素材は落ち着いた雰囲気を出す)
● マットな	matte	Matte finishing gives a soft impression. (マットな仕上げは優しい印象を与える)

Activity Guide
Material

● 光沢のある	glossy, shiny	I added a glossy finish to the table. （テーブルに光沢のある仕上げを施した）
● つるつるした	smooth	Smooth surfaces do not smudge easily. （つるつるした表面は汚れがつきにくい）
● ざらざらした	rough, grained	In this case, the rough texture gives a sense of luxury. （この場合、ざらざらした質感が高級感を与えている）
● でこぼこした	bumpy	We need a strategy to reduce the noise caused by this bumpy roads. （でこぼこした道路による騒音を減らすために対策が必要だ）
● シボをつける	add texturing	By adding texturing to the surface, you can avoid slipping. （表面にシボ加工をすることですべり止めになる）
● キラキラした	sparkling, glittering	I want it to glitter like a sparkling star. （キラキラした星のような感じにしたい）
● ぎらぎらした	glaring	The light coming in through the car windshield created a glaring reflection. （車のフロントガラスから入る光がぎらぎら反射した）
● 温かみのある	with warmth	Wood with a sense of warmth is appropriate for the parts that people hold onto and sit on. （握ったり座ったりする部分には温かみのある木材がふさわしい）
● 木製の	wooden	Wodden tables stain easily. （木製のテーブルはシミがつきやすい）
● 布張りの	upholstered	Upholstered furniture is very popular. （布張りの家具は人気がある）
● 目地を強調する	emphasize the joint	With a relatively large wall, I want a design that emphasizes the pattern of the joints. （比較的大きな壁面は目地を強調したデザインにしたい）
● ブツブツした	bubbling, pimply	The bubbling surface is the outstanding feature. （ブツブツした表面が目立つ特徴になっている）
● ツヤが有り過ぎ／無さ過ぎ	too shiny/less shiny	If it's too shiny or not shiny enough, it can reduce the feeling of luxury. （ツヤが有り過ぎても無さ過ぎても高級感につながらないことがある）
● 滑らかな	smooth, clean	The smooth connection gives it a gentle feel. （滑らかなつながりが優しい感じを作る）

Activity Guide
Material

● 流れのある	flowing, elegant	This texture has a flowing form that matches well. (この素材感が流れるようなフォルムにマッチしている)
● ザックリした	rough-hewn	The rough-hewn feel combines appearance with protection against cold. (ザックリした風合いが見た目にも防寒にも役立っている)
● 凹凸のある	uneven	An uneven finish seems to reduce the sense of cheapness. (凹凸のある仕上げが安っぽさを軽減しているようだ)
● ゴワゴワした	coarse	A stiff or coarse appearance is successful in creating a strong and robust image. (堅くゴワゴワした表情が堅牢なイメージにつながり成功している)
● 素材感のある	textured	The surface has a textured quality to it. (表面は触り心地に素材感がある品質だ)
● 高級感	luxury	Luxury is a vague concept, but it is one of the most important conditions when creating products. (高級感は曖昧な概念ではあるが、製品作りには大切な条件の一つとなる)
● 上質感のある	high-quality, excellent	By using high-quality materials appropriately it's possible to create a balance between cost and a sense of quality. (適宜上質感のある素材を使うことでコストと質感とのバランスを産み出すことができる)
● 安っぽい	cheap, low	I've made it lighter, but in a way that doesn't make it look cheap. (軽量化が安っぽさにならないように工夫している)
● モコモコした	shaggy, hairy	I want a coat with a shaggy collar. (モコモコした襟のコートが欲しい)
● ふさふさの(毛でおおわれた)	furry	The furry rabbits are cute. (ふさふさした毛の兎はかわいい)
● 肌触りの良さ	soft feel	A nice finish and a soft feel is particularly important for consumer electronics and beauty products. (特に家電や美容製品などには肌触りの良い仕上げが不可欠だ)
● 触れたくなる	make you want to touch, be tempted to touch	with a finish that, at first glance, makes you want to touch it (一見、触れてみたくなるような風合いの仕上がり)
● 触り心地の優しさ	soft to the touch	Being soft to the touch stimulates the desire to buy it. (触り心地の良さが購買意欲を刺激する)

Activity Guide
Material

● すべすべした	smooth, sleek	Realize not only the look but an actual smooth feel. (見た目だけでなく実際にすべすべした感触を実現させなさい)
● きめの粗い	coarse	Evoke a casual feel via coarse facial expressions. (きめの粗い表情でカジュアルな感じを出しなさい)
● さらさら(感)の	smooth	It has a smooth, dry feeling on the skin that is especially popular in summer. (肌へのさらさら感は特に夏場に求められる)
● クッション性のある	cushioned, padded, with pad	It's an idea for a cushioned sofa that has the right material in the right place. (素材を適材適所に配したクッション性のあるソファーの提案だ)
● 椅子のクッション性を良くする	pad a chair	The chair needs to have more padding to be considered comfortable. (椅子は快適性のためにクッション性を良くする必要がある)
● ひけ	imperfection	Products with imperfections will be rejected during the quality control inspection. (ひけの有る製品は品質検査で不合格となる)

行為

● ～を(布)で巻く	wrap (cloth) around	Combine a sense of quality and usability by wrapping leather around the handle. (持ち手に皮を巻くことで上質感と使い勝手を両立させなさい)
● 皮を貼る	put leather	Putting leather around the handle gives it a regal look. (皮を貼ったハンドルは豪華に見える)
● ～の見栄えを良くする	refurbish	By refurbishing it, you can ask for a higher price. (見栄え良くすることで高い値付けが可能である)
● ～をピカピカに磨く	polish (up), furbish	The wood of that chair may be old but it should polish up nicely. (その椅子の木部は古いがよく手入れがされていてピカピカだ)

177

Activity Guide
Material

その他

- 射出成型   injection molding   Injection molding is good for mass production.
  （射出成型は大量生産にむいている）

- 真空成型   vacuum molding   Vacuum molding has become an inexpensive way to make shapes.
  （真空成型は成型の安価な方法だ）

- ブロー成形（ダブルブロー成形）   blow molding (double blow)   Blow molding is widely used in making musical instrument cases.
  （ブロー成形は楽器のケースを作るときに多用されている）

- コンクリート打ち放し、ボード等   exposed concrete   Many art schools seem to favor the look of exposed concrete.
  （多くのアートスクールではコンクリート打ち放しの外観が好まれるようだ）

Activity Guide
Operation

操作

- ボタンを押す | push/press the button | Push the button on the right.
（向かって右のボタンを押しなさい）

- スイッチを入れる | flip the switch | Flip the switch to turn on the power.
（スイッチを入れて電源を入れなさい）

- ダイヤルをひねる | twist the dial | Twist the dial on the timer clockwise.
（タイマーのダイヤルを時計回りにひねりなさい）

- ノブを引く | pull the knob | Pull the knob to unlock.
（ノブを引いて開錠しなさい）

- リモコンを振る | shake the remote control | The signal is sent automatically by shaking the remote control.
（リモコンを振ることで自動的に信号が送られる）

- 〜を回転させる | rotate | Turn off the water by rotating the container.
（容器を回転させることで水を切りなさい）

- （車体を）傾ける | lean in | The bike rider leaned in as he turned the corner.
（ライダーはコーナーを曲がる時に車体を傾けた）

- 機能を選択する | select a function | You can select a function with your fingertips.
（指先で機能を選択できる）

- その都度切り替える | adjust each time | The radio can be adjusted each time.
（ラジオはその都度切り替えられる）

- 〜を調節する | adjust | How do you adjust the drill speed?
（どうやって回転速度を調節するのですか）

- 〜をセットする | set | Set the radio.
（ラジオをセットしなさい）

- 〜を開け放つ | leave ... open | Leave the window open for ventilation.
（換気のため窓を開けなさい）

- 〜を運転する | drive | It is a lot of fun to drive this car.
（車を運転することはとても楽しい）

- 〜を動かす | drive | Steam drives the engine.
（蒸気がエンジンを動かす）

- 〜を点灯する | turn on, illuminate | Turn on the lights in the evening.
（夕方にはライトを点灯しなさい）

Activity Guide
Operation

● ～を直感的に理解する（取説不要の）	understand ... intuitively (not refer to the manual)	Recently, game controls are understood intuitively. （最新のゲーム機は直感的に理解できる）

行為

● ～をひっくり返す	turn ... upside-down	Turn the canoe upside-down when you are not using it. （カヌーを使わないときはひっくり返しなさい）
	rotate	This image is upside-down. We need to rotate it. （この画像はさかさまだ。ひっくり返す必要がある）
● 仰向けに寝る	lie on one's back	Please climb into the bed and lie on your back. （ベッドに仰向けに寝てください）
● うつぶせに寝る	lie on one's stomach, lie prone	Operate while lying on one's stomach. （うつ伏せに寝て操作しなさい）
● ハンドルを握る	grab hold of the handle	Grab hold of the handle firmly. （力を入れてハンドルを握りなさい）
● 靴を履く	put on one's shoes	Put on your shoes in the entrance hall. （玄関で靴を履きなさい）
● 呼吸する	breathe	The greenery makes the whole building seem like it is breathing. （緑化により建物全体がまるで呼吸しているようだ）
● グローブをつける	wear/put on gloves	Wear gloves so your hands don't slip. （滑らないようグローブをつけなさい）
● ～を収納する	store	Store it under the floor. （床下に収納しなさい）
● ～を縮める	draw in, shrink	Draw in your arms and legs. （手足を縮めなさい）
● ～を伸ばす	stretch	Stretch the exercise band as far as possible. （エクササイズバンドを思い切り伸ばしなさい）
● ～を折りたたむ	fold	Fold up the tripod. （三脚を折りたたみなさい）

Activity Guide
Operation

● ～を広げる	spread, widen	Spread the map on the desk. (机に地図を広げなさい)
● ～を注ぐ	pour	Pour the hot water. (熱いお湯を注ぎなさい)
● ～を展開する	expand, display, develop	Expand the luggage compartment by changing the seating arrangement. (シートの配列を変えて荷室を展開しなさい)

行為の誘発

● ～に滞留する	stop and hang out	There's also a place to stop and hang out. (滞留するスペースもある)
● A から B へ移動する	move from A to B	Move from above ground to underground. (地上から地下へ移動しなさい)
● ～を通って	through	Move to the pavilion through the courtyard. (中庭を通って東屋へ移動しなさい)
● アクティビティを誘発する	encourage activity	We need a gimmick to encourage activity. (アクティビティを誘発するような仕掛けが必要だ)
● 目線が行きかう	several lines of sight	Several lines of sight are available to the shoppers. (買い物客の目線が行きかう)
● 目線が届く範囲	field of vision	It will be displayed within salespeople's field of vision. (それは店員の目線が届く範囲に展示されるだろう)
● 回遊する	circulate	The terrace was designed for shoppers to circulate around. (テラスは買い物客が回遊するように設計されている)
● 出入りができる	can come and go	You can come and go from any direction. (どの方向からも出入りができる)
● ～に出られる	can leave	You can leave the forest from this secret exit. (秘密の抜け道から森に出られる)

Activity Guide
Composition

行為

● ~をセンター合わせにする	place ... on the center line	The vertically aligned buttons should be placed on the center line. (縦に並ぶボタンは、センター合わせに配列すべきだ)	
● ~を右揃えにする	align ... to the right	Try aligning everything to the right. (全てを右揃えにして並べてみてください)	
● ~を下揃えにする	align ... at the bottom	Let's look at the differences in height after they are aligned at the bottom. (下揃えにして高さの違いを見てみよう)	
● ハイライト(エッジ)を入れる	add a highlight	Let's add highlights to the surface to give it better balance. (バランスを良くするために表面にハイライトを入れてみよう)	
● 強弱をつける	add contrast	This is too vague. Why don't we add more contrast? (ぼやっとしているから、もっと強弱をつけたらどうかな)	
● ~にアクセントをつける	accentuate	I think it accentuates the entire structure. (それが全体構成にアクセントをつけていると思う)	
● 粗密をつける	add density	Because it's flat overall, why don't we make a change and add some density? (全体に平坦な感じだから、もっと疎密をつけて変化を出したら)	
● パンチを効かせる	add punch	It's so safe that it's boring. Let's add some punch. (無難でつまらないんだよ。もっとパンチを効かせよう)	
	give ... a twist	Why don't you use red to give it a twist? (なぜ赤でパンチを効かせないの)	
● ~を線で囲む	border ... with lines	I've separated the categories by bordering them with lines. (線で囲んでカテゴリわけをしました)	
● ~を反転する	flip over	By making a mirror image of one side and flipping it over to the other side, we can make a perfectly symmetrical model. (片面の鏡像をもう一方に反転させると左右対称の形に見せることができる)	
● 素材を組み合わせる	combine the materials	Combine the materials to create something interesting. (素材を組み合わせて面白みを出しなさい)	
● ~を配置する	arrange, lay out	I arranged the buttons in a row. (ボタンを横一列に並べて配置しました)	

Activity Guide
Composition

● ～を離して配置する	space ... apart	Please space the tables farther apart. （テーブルを少し離して配置してください）
● ～を離す	move ... (farther) away	Please move it farther away to make more space. （それをもっと遠くに離して空間を確保してください）
● 間隔を合わせる	adjust the spacing	We adjusted the spacing of the windows to offer a sense of unity. （窓の間隔を合わせて統一感を出した）
● (色)面積のバランスをとる	maintain (color) balance	Instead of putting this line in, erase the other line to maintain the overall balance. （この線を入れる代わりに、他の線を消して全体のバランスをとってください） Why don't you add more blue for better balance with the other colors. （もっと青い部分を増やして他の色とのバランスをとってはどうか）
● ～を分散する	break down	Breaking it down into several specific points would be more efficient. （ポイントをいくつかに分散した方が効果的だ）
● ～を反復する	repeat	Repeating the same theme gives a sense of unity. （同じテーマを反復することにより統一感が出る）
● ～を統一する	unify	The images of the two models are unified into one. （2つの機種のイメージは1つに統一されている）

状況・状態

● 片側	one side	Because it's symmetric, only one side of the model was made. （左右対称なので、モデルの片面だけ作った）
● 構図がよい	well composed	This picture is well composed. （この絵は構図がよい）
● (要素が多すぎて)ビジーになる	look crowded	Don't all of the highlights make this shape look crowded? （この形はハイライトが多すぎてビジーじゃないかな）
● ○階建て	○ stories high	This building is 45 stories high. （このビルは45階建てである）

Activity Guide
Composition

●	明快な架構	straightforward construction	We want to show the simple, straightforward construction of this building. (この建物の明快な架構を見せたい)
●	架構の美しさ	beauty of the structure	The steel-frame roof and unfinished ceiling bring out the beauty of the structure. (屋根は鉄骨造で天井をはらず、架構の美しさを見せている)
●	しっかりした骨格	sturdy structure	You could say that the sturdy structure has an image of reliability. (しっかりした骨格は安心感があると言える)
●	きついウエッジ	sharp wedge	Overall, the sharp wedge of this car makes it appear busy. (この車は全体にウエッジがキツく落ち着かない)
●	まとまり感	a sense of unity	The close proximity of hue and saturation offers a sense of color unity. (近い色相や彩度が色のまとまり感を出している)
●	まとまっている	well organized	It is well organized as it is. (このままでよくまとまっている)
●	バラバラ感	a disjointed/ scattered feeling	The difference in treatment gives it a disjointed feeling. (処理の違いがバラバラ感を出している)
●	空疎な感じ	a sense of emptiness	The lack of pillars in this space gives it a sense of emptiness. (これだけの空間に柱がないと空疎な感じがする)
●	密度感のある（ぎゅっと詰まった）	tightly packed	The narrow site had a tightly packed design. (狭い敷地に密度感のある設計を行った)
●	分割した面	divided surface	The divided surface of the outer wall is a new look. (外壁の面を分割した見せ方が新しい)
●	緊張感のある	tense	The balanced use of space projects a tense composition. (間のバランスのよさで緊張感のある構成にしている)
●	間がもたない	a poor use of space	Using only one picture on a such a huge wall is a poor use of space. (この広い壁に絵が一枚だけでは間が持たない)
●	間	space	The emptiness adds a sense of value to the space. (何も付け加えないことで間を感じさせる)
●	黄金比	golden ratio	The car has been designed based on the golden ratio. (車は黄金比に基づいてデザインされている)

Activity Guide
Composition

●	基本寸法 （モジュール）で 構成された	basic-sized	Most rooms have basic-sized built-in drawers. （ほとんどの部屋に基本寸法で構成された造り付けの棚がある）
●	浮遊感	a light, airy feeling, a floating feeling	The use of transparent materials in the construction projected a light, airy feeling. （透明素材をもちいて構成し浮遊感を出している）
●	交差する	intersect	The various intersecting lines are a characteristic of his works. （たくさんの線の交差が彼の作品の特徴である）
●	斜めに	diagonally	The buttons were arranged diagonally toward the upper right side. （右上に向かってボタンを斜めに並べた）
●	縦に	vertically	Please arrange the lights vertically from the front in order to lead visitors to the back. （訪問者を奥へと導くために手前から縦に照明を並べてください）
●	横に	side by side	Arrange side by side to make it easy to see. （見やすいように横に並べなさい）
●	位置	position	The handle position makes it easy to use. （ハンドルの位置が使いやすい）
●	前後	the front and the back	Let's put the instructions on both the front and the back of the model. （モデルの前後に注意書きを出そう）
●	上下	up and down, vertically	There is something not right about the vertical line that is separated up and down. （上下に分割された縦のラインが気になる）
●	立体的に展開する	unfold vertically as well as horizontally	The greenery from the entrance unfolds vertically as well as horizontally into the courtyard and roof. （エントランスの緑が中庭や屋上へと立体的に展開している）
●	○個のゾーンに分けられた	be divided into ○ zones	This facility was divided into three special zones for play, study, and hanging out. （この施設は、遊び、学習、集いの3つのゾーンに分けられている）
●	字間	character spacing	Adjust the character spacing. （字間を調整しなさい）
●	多層からなる	multi-layered	This shopping mall was designed to focus on its multi-layered terrace. （そのショッピングモールは多層からなるテラスを中心に設計された）

Activity Guide
Composition

● 密集した	dense	Behind the station, there is a dense concentration of old houses. （駅裏は古い家屋が密集している）
● リズム感	a certain rhythm	The entire building is constructed with a certain rhythm. （建物全体がリズム感のある構成となっている）
● 直交している	meeting at right angles	Beams meeting at right angles give a sense of strength. （直交する梁が力強さを出している）
● A と B からなる （構成された）	be constructed with A and B	This building is constructed with aluminum and wood. （この建物はアルミと木からなる）
● ～と調和のとれた	harmonize with	The building harmonizes with the surrounding area. （この建物は周囲と調和がとれている）
● 良いバランス	good balance	We want a plant design with good balance. （バランスの良い植栽計画を求めている）
● ～と相似の	analogous to	The buttons were designed to be analogous to the indicators. （ボタンはメーターと相似の形で計画された）
● ～の○倍の	○ times the size of	It has ballooned to three times the size of the original. （元の大きさの３倍に膨れ上がった）
● ～と比例関係の	in proportion to/with	The budget is in proportion to the size of the house. （予算は家の大きさと比例関係である）
● 対称形の	symmetrical	The symmetrical construction has an indescribable calm. （対称形の建築は何とも言えない落ち着きがある）
● 非対称の	asymmetrical	An asymmetrical plan with many curves catches the eye. （曲線を多用した非対称のプランが目を引く）
● 対比	contrast	The contrast between light and dark in this picture is too strong. （この写真は光と影の対比が強すぎる）
● 幅と高さの関係	width and height relationship	The width and height relationship of that table is strange. （その机は幅と高さの関係が変だ）
● 縦横の比率	lengthwise and crosswise ratio	You should reconsider the lengthwise and crosswise ratio. （縦横の比率を見直した方が良い）
	vertical and horizontal ratio	Let's reverse the vertical and horizontal ratio and have a look. （縦横の比率を逆転させて見てみよう）

Activity Guide
Composition

- 水平と垂直の関係   horizontal and vertical relationship   Nothing is more basic than the horizontal and vertical relationship.
（水平と垂直の関係が何よりも基本である）

- 面積比   area ratio, ratio of area   The area ratio is not balanced enough.
（面積比のバランスが今一つだね）

Activity Guide
Sense

感情（快／不快／穏やか／驚き）

快

● わくわくした	excited	I want to design a product that makes people excited. （人々をわくわくさせる製品をデザインしたい）
● やる気にさせる	be motivating for	This device is motivating for players. （この仕掛けでプレイヤーをやる気にさせる）
● 楽しい	enjoyable, fun, pleasant	Driving is enjoyable. Driving is a fun hobby. （車を運転することは楽しい。ドライブは楽しい趣味だ）
● さわやかな	refreshing, bracing	For the summer sales release, we want to provide refreshing colors. （夏に発売されるアイテムは、さわやかな色合いにしたい）
● 清々しい	fresh, refreshing	Use the clean image of white to give a feeling of a fresh morning. （清々しい朝の感じを演出するために清潔感のある白いイメージを使いなさい）
● 親近感を持つ	familiar	Robots that need a little help are more familiar to people. （手助けを必要とするロボットに親近感を持つ）
● 懐かしい感じがする	evoke fond memories	The music evoked fond memories. （懐かしい感じのする音楽だ）
● 懐かしい	nostalgic	My nostalgic emotional attachment inspired me to create this design. （懐かしい想いからこのデザインを発想しました）
● 仲良くなる	make/become friends	You can make new friends through using this product. （この製品を通して新しい人と仲良くなることができる）
● カジュアルな	casual	How about using denim in order to suggest a casual feeling? （カジュアルな雰囲気を出すためにデニムを使ってはどうかな）
● しっくりくる	go well with	That shirt goes well with your eyes. （あのシャツはあなたの瞳の色にしっくりくる）
	fit nicely	Using this color here fits nicely. （ここにこの色を置くとしっくりくる）

188

Activity Guide
Sense

● 開放感	a sense/feeling of openness, openness	Widening the entrance gives a greater sense of openness. （開口部を広く取りより開放感を出す）
● 安心感	a sense of security	Bigger legs give a sense of security. （大きめの脚部が安心感を与えている）
		Double locks on the entrance door give a sense of security. （玄関ドアの二重ロックが安心感を与える）
● イケてる	cool	That's a cool shirt. （そのシャツ、イケてるね）
● 清潔感	a sense of cleanliness	The color scheme in the bathroom should evoke a sense of cleanliness. （トイレの色彩計画は清潔感を出すべきだ）
● 情熱的な	passionate	For today's show, let's go with passionate red lipstick. （今日のショーは、情熱的な赤い口紅でいこう）
● 洗練された	elegant	The narrow logo type gives the product an elegant feeling. （細いロゴは製品に洗練された印象を与える）
● 高揚感	a sense of excitement	Use a vivid color scheme to express a sense of excitement. （ヴィヴィッドな色遣いで高揚感を表現しなさい）

....

不快

● 腑に落ちない、納得がいかない	hard to figure out/understand, doubt	Requiring this operation here again makes it hard to figure out. （ここでもう一度この操作を要求するのは腑に落ちない）
● 不安になる	feel uneasy/anxious	Not knowing the final destinations makes operators feel uneasy. （到達点が不明のままではオペレーターが不安になる）
● 心地良くない	feel uncomfortable	Wearing a suit always makes me feel uncomfortable. （スーツを着るといつも心地良くない）
● 怖い	intimidating	The sharp edges are intimidating. （先端の尖った形が怖い）
● 危険を感じる	sense the danger	The workers intuitively sensed the danger of operating the machine. （従業員は直感的に機械のその操作に危険を感じた）

Activity Guide
Sense

● うるさい（騒音）	noisy, loud	The exhaust coming from the car was noisy. （車の排気音がうるさかった）
● うるさい（気になる）	busy, noisy	This line makes this composition look too busy. （この線のおかげで構成がとてもうるさくなっている）
● いらいらする	be frustrated	The pilots were frustrated by the lack of usability. （操縦者は操作性の悪さにいらいらした）
● 暗い	dark, gloomy	Hearing bad news puts people in a dark mood. （不幸なニュースを聞くと暗い気持ちになる）
● 狭苦しい（せせこましい）	crowded, busy	Adding too many elements gives the impression of it being too crowded. （あまり要素を増やすとせせこましい印象になってしまうよ）
● 閉鎖的な	enclosed, exclusive, closed	Enclosed spaces are suffocating. （閉鎖的な空間にいると息が詰まる）

穏やか

● 落ち着く	calm	Create a sense of calm by using natural materials. （天然素材を用いて落ち着いた感じにしなさい）
	relaxed	I want to design a relaxed space. （落ち着いた空間にデザインしたい）
	less busy, composed	We should replace one of the colors with white to make it less busy. （落ち着かせるために一色を白に置き換えるべきだ）
● リラックスした	relaxed	I want to evoke a relaxed atmosphere. （リラックスした雰囲気を演出したい）
● 落ち着いた（リラックスした）	relaxing	How about using a slightly darker color to create a relaxing atmosphere? （落ち着いた印象を与えるために少し暗めの色を使ったらどうかな）
● 優しい	soft, gentle	I like towels with a soft texture. （優しい肌触りのタオルが好きだ）
● 〜を和らげる	ease, lessen	We can ease frustration by eliminating steps from the process. （手順を減らすことでイライラ感を和らげることができる）

Activity Guide

Sense

● 和む	soothing	Watching a cute character is soothing. (かわいいキャラクターを見ると心が和む)
● 癒される	be calmed	The attendants were calmed by the scent of cypress in the room. (来場者は部屋のヒノキの香りに癒された)
● ほっとさせる(安心させる)	comforting	The feeling of the product is comforting for users. (その製品の感触はユーザーをほっとさせる)
● 親しみやすい	friendly	Small scooters are friendly to women. (小さなスクーターは女性に親しみやすい)
● より親しみやすい	friendlier	I would like to design this big bike to be friendlier to women. (この大型バイクは女性により親しみやすいデザインにしたい)
● ゆったりとした	less cramped, less complexed	Sparsely furnishing the narrow space projects a spacious image, making it appear less cramped. (狭い空間でも少なめの家具を配置することで広いイメージを出しゆったりとした空間に感じさせる。)

驚き

● 〜を驚かす	surprise	This product surprised consumers. (その製品は人々に驚きをもたらした)
	shock	The new technology shocked the bicycle industry. (その新技術は自転車業界に驚きをもたらした)
● 驚くべき	astonishing	This product achieved an astonishing evolution. (この製品は驚くべき進化を遂げました)
	startling	Scientists have made several startling discoveries. (科学者たちは驚くべき発見をした)
	marvelous	My new computer has many marvelous new features. (私の新しいコンピューターは驚くほどの新しい機能を備えている)
	amazing	Our product uses an amazing new technology. (我々の製品は驚くべき新技術を使用している)
	wonderful	Let me introduce you to our wonderful new product. (我々の驚くべき新製品を紹介させてください)

Activity Guide
Sense

● ～にはっと気づく	It suddenly makes me aware of	It suddenly made me aware of things I hadn't noticed before. （今まで気づいていなかったことにはっと気づかされた）
	realize	I realized many things about myself after my girlfriend dumped me. （僕は彼女にふられてから自分自身の多くのことにはっと気づいた）
● 目の覚めるような	eye-opening	It was an eye-opening experience to be part of the team. （そのチームで働いたことは、目の覚めるような経験だった）

印象

● 美しい	beautiful, lovely	Your wife is not only beautiful, she is also a lovely person. （君の奥さんは美しいだけでなく、性格もすてきだね）
● 活気のある	bustling, lively, energetic	There are many stylish bars in the bustling area of the town. （その街の繁華街にはお洒落なバーがたくさんある）
● 先進的な	advanced	The new bullet train has an advanced shape. （新しい新幹線は先進的な形状だ）
● 速そうな	a sense of speed, look fast	Inserting sharp highlights that evoke a sense of speed creates a fast-looking image. （スピード感のあるシャープなハイライトを入れて速そうなイメージを出す）
● かっこいい	cool	The watch that he bought yesterday is really cool. （彼が昨日買った腕時計は実にかっこいい）
	sharp	You look sharp in that car. （あの車に乗った君はかっこいいね）
	trendy	She always wears trendy clothes. （彼女はいつもかっこいい服を着ている）
	hip, trendy	We want to choose a hip design popular with young people. （若い人に人気のあるかっこいいデザインを選びたい）
● ～をかわいい感じにする	make ... cute	I want to make it cute by rounding the head. （頭をまるっこくしてかわいい感じにしたい）
● 立体感を出す	create a sense of three dimensions	By adding shadowing, I want to create a sense of three dimensions. （影を入れて、立体感を出したい）

Activity Guide: Sense

● 透明感をつける	add a sense of transparency	I want to add more of a sense of transparency in the overlapping part. （重なり部分にもっと透明感を出したい）
● 派手な	flashy	This glittering color is too flashy and creates a vulgar impression. （このギラギラした色が派手すぎて下品な印象だね）
		A flashy appearance excites the spectators. （ど派手な登場で観衆をわかせる）
	gaudy	He wore a gaudy necktie to a party. （彼は派手なネクタイをパーティーで身に着けていた）
	flamboyant	The young man looked flamboyant in his flashy sports car. （派手なスポーツカーに乗った若い男はけばけばしくみえた）
	garish	I thought wearing a bowtie to school a little garish. （学校に蝶ネクタイはすこし派手だと思った）
● 明らかな、目立つ	glaring	I found a glaring error. （明らかな間違いを見つけた）
● 大人っぽさ	adulthood and maturity	A chic suit gives the impression of adulthood and maturity. （シックなスーツは大人っぽい印象を与える）
● 緻密感	attention to detail	a product with small, well-finished parts that looks like it was made with great attention to detail （小さなパーツの仕上がりまで気を配られた緻密感のある製品）
● プレミアム感	a sense of premiumness	Use genuine leather to bring out a sense of premiumness. （プレミアム感を出すために本革を採用しなさい）

Activity Guide
Scale

縮尺・寸法・図面

●	～を2倍寸で描く	draw ... in double scale	Draw the details of the handle in double scale. (取っ手の詳細は2倍寸で描きなさい)
●	～を1/2スケールで描く	draw ... in a half scale	Draw a pot in a half or one-third scale. (鍋を1/2または1/3スケールで描きなさい)
●	原寸(図)	full scale/full size (drawing),	Draw a handle in a full scale. (取っ手は原寸図で描きなさい)
●	原寸、実際の大きさ	actual size, full size	It appears large on the drawing, but its actual size is only 1cm. (図面では大きく見えるが、実際の大きさは1cmしかない)
●	1/100の縮尺	scale of one to one hundred	This drawing is made on a scale of one to one hundred. (この図面は1/100の縮尺で描かれている)
●	縮尺は何分の1ですか？	What is the scale of ...?	What is the scale of this drawing to? (この図面の縮尺は何分の1ですか)
●	何分の1の縮尺で表現する？	What scale should we reduce ...?	What scale should we reduce the drawing to? (何分の1の縮尺の図面で表現しますか)
●	詳細においては	with regard to the level of detail	With regard to the level of detail, we are able to see the rounded edges. (詳細においては、端部の丸みがわかる)
●	(詳細)模型（図面)では	in a (detailed) model (drawings)	In a detailed model, you are able to see the fine points of the corners. (詳細模型では、角の細部まで確認できる)
●	全体模型で	in the overall/complete model	The composition can be confirmed by checking the overall model. (全体模型で構成を確認することができる)
●	原寸模型で	from a full scale model, from a mock-up	I will confirm the size of the chamfer from the full scale model. (角の面取り寸法の大きさは原寸模型で確認する)
●	ブイチであたる（ざっくり寸法を測る）	be measured as ...	The drawing was measured as 50mm, but actually it should be 48mm. (図面をブイチであたると50mmだが、実際は48mmのはずだ)
●	○の幅／高さ	wide/high	The table is 750mm wide/high. (机の幅／高さは750mmだ)

194

Activity Guide
Scale

● ～の幅／高さを測ると○だ	If we measure the ..., it is ○ wide/high	If we measure the table, it is 750mm wide/high. （机を測ると、750mmの幅／高さだ）
● 書きこみ寸法	figured dimensions	We prioritized the figured dimensions. （書き込み寸法で示された数値を優先した）
● 寸法を記載する	write down the dimensions	Write down the dimensions from the center line. （中心線からの寸法を記載しなさい）
● 長さを記載する	write down the length	Write down the maximum length of the product. （製品の最大長を記載しなさい）
● 寸法線	dimension line	You have to mark the dimension line clearly. （寸法線はわかりやすく書くべきだ）
● 芯々○mの間隔で	spaced ○ meters from one center to the next	houses spaced 5 meters from one center to the next （芯々5m間隔で並ぶ家）
● ○mの間隔を置いて	spaced ○ meters apart	houses spaced 5 meters apart （5mの間隔を置いて建つ家）
● 等間隔で	at equal spaces	Put lights at equal spaces（of 3 meters）. （照明を等間隔（3m間隔）に配置しなさい）
● ～を手描きで描く	draw ... oneself	You'll draw it yourself? （手描きでかくつもりですか）
● 手描き図	hand drawn	hand drawn, half-size （1/2の手描き図）
● CAD図	CAD drawn	CAD drawn, half-size （1/2のCAD図）

比較

● スケール感	a sense of scale	I can't understand the sense of scale of the actual car from this sketch. （このスケッチでは実車のスケール感がわからない）
● 大きさ感（そのモノらしい大きさ感）	magnitude	We can't grasp the magnitude because the perspective was overemphasized. （オーバーパースがきつくて大きさ感が出ていない）

Activity Guide
Scale

●	～ぐらいの大きさ（～にちょうどいい大きさ）	be appropriate as/for	The size is appropriate for a wristwatch. （それは腕時計としてちょうどいい大きさだ）
●	片手に収まる	fit in one hand	The digital camera should fit in one hand. （デジタルカメラは片手に収まる大きさがいい）
●	～と同一のスケール感	the same sense of scale as	This building has the same sense of scale as the neighbouring houses. （この建物は周辺の住宅と同一のスケール感だ）
●	～から突出する（スケール感）	protrude from, stick out	This building is protruding from the neighbouring houses. （この建物は周辺の住宅から突出したスケール感だ）
●	～と馴染む（スケール感）	go together with, match	This building goes together with the neighbouring houses. （この建物は周辺の住宅と馴染んだスケール感だ）

関連手法

●	詳細に至るまで	in detail, down to the smallest detail	Consider everything in detail. （詳細に至るまで全て検討しなさい）
●	大きな規模の（ボリューム）	large-scale (volume)	According to this plan, the volume will be large scale. （この計画だと、大きな規模のボリュームになる）
●	～を細やかに分割する	break up ... into tiny parts	Let's break up the volume into tiny parts. （ボリュームを細やかに分割しよう）
●	～を分ける（～に分ける）	divide up, (divide into)	Let's divide up the building (into three parts) to reduce the volume. （棟を（3つの部分に）分けて建物のボリュームを抑えよう）
●	～を区切る	separate	Let's separate the facility into smaller buildings to reduce the size. （棟を小さく区切って、建物のボリュームを抑えよう）
●	遠くからは	from a distance, from faraway	From a distance, we can see the tower, but from nearby we can recognize the lower part of the building. （遠くからは、塔が見えるが、近くでは建物の低層部が認識される）
●	近くでは	from close up, from near	From close up, we can get a better view of the water. （近くでは、水景をよりよく見ることができる）

Activity Guide: Situation

シチュエーション（時間・状況／場所）

時間・状況

- 移動中に（表示面が動く場合） — in motion — This display is easy to look at while in motion.
（この画面は動きがあっても見やすい）

- 移動中に（見る側も動いている場合） — in motion — This display is easy to look at while you are in motion.
（この表示は（車で）移動している最中でも見やすい）

- 通勤中に — on the way to work — I like to read books on the train on the way to work.
（私は通勤中に本を読むのが好きだ）

- 食事中 — mealtimes — We should choose lighting equipment that is suitable for mealtimes.
（食事に適した照明を選択した方がよい）

- 1960年代に — in the (nineteen) sixties — The stylistic elements of this design was popular in the sixties.
（このデザインの傾向は60年代に流行ったものだ）

- 人混みで — in crowds — The sound of this speaker is clear, even in crowds.
（このスピーカーの音は人混みの中でも聞き取りやすい）

- 水中で — underwater, in the water — This watch was made to be used underwater.
（この時計は水中で使うことを想定して作られた）

場所

- 街中で — in the city — This car drives smoothly in the city.
（街中でこの車は快適に走行する）

- 田舎で — in the countryside — This car is perfect for weekend drives in the countryside.
（この車は田舎での週末ドライブにいい）

- 高速道路で — on the highway — This car runs smoothly on the highway.
（この車は高速道路で安定して走行する）

- 路上で — on a street — Recharging terminals for electric cars are available on several streets in London.
（ロンドンの多くの路上で電気自動車の充電ターミナルが利用できる）

Activity Guide
Situation

● 観光地で	at sightseeing areas	The signs at sightseeing areas should be easy for everyone to understand. (観光地で使うサインは誰が見てもわかりやすくするべきだ)
● 狭い場所で	in a small area	In a small area, the height of the ceiling should be carefully decided. (狭い場所では、天井の高さを慎重に決定する必要がある)
● オープンスペースで	in an open space	The new park is an open space where people are free to let their dogs run loose. (新しい公園は犬を自由に放すことができるオープンスペースだ)
● パブリック(な場所)	the public (space)	I will try to design a garden that is open to the public. (パブリックな場所に向けて開かれた庭をデザインしたい)
● プライベートな場所	the private space	This part of the library is a private study space. (図書館のこの部分はプライベートな勉強室だ)
● プライバシーを保つ	maintain a sense of privacy	Natural impediments block the view of the public space, allowing it to maintain a sense of privacy. (公共空間の視線を自然に遮ることで、プライバシーを保つことができる)

ロケーション (場所・位置／周辺との関係／高低・勾配)

場所・位置

● ～に設置する(された)	place (be placed)	
屋外に設置する(された)	place outside	This light is meant to be placed outside. (この照明は屋外に設置することを想定している)
天井に設置する(された)	place on the ceiling	This light is meant to be placed on the ceiling. (この照明は天井に設置することを想定している)
壁に設置する(された)	place on the wall	This light is meant to be placed on the wall. (この照明は壁に設置することを想定している)
● ～の中心に(中央に)	at the center of	It is located at the center of the city. (都市の中心部に位置している)

Activity Guide
Situation

● ~の端部に	at the edge of, at the tip of	It is located at the edge of the city.	（都市部の端部に位置している）
● ~に隣接して	adjacent to	The site is adjacent to the residential area.	（敷地は住宅地に隣接している）
● ~に面して	facing	The site is facing the residential area.	（敷地は住宅地に面している）
● ~に近い	near	The site is near the residential area.	（敷地は住宅地に近い）
● ~を見渡す	command	The house commands a view of the whole town.	（その家は街全体を見渡している）
● 見晴らしが良い	have a fine view	This terrace has a fine view.	（このテラスは見晴らしが良い）
● ~を見下ろす	look over	The view of the house looks over the whole town.	（その家は街全体を見下ろしている）
● ~を見上げる	look upwards	The site looks upwards toward the mountains.	（敷地は山を見上げる場所にある）
● ~に位置する	be located		
緑豊かな環境に位置する	be located in a leafy neighbourhood	The site is located in a leafy neighbourhood.	（敷地は緑豊かな環境に位置している）
都市部に位置する	be located in the urban area	The site is located in the urban area.	（敷地は都市部に位置している）
住宅地に位置する	be located in a residental area	The site is located in a residential area.	（敷地は住宅地に位置している）
○階に位置する	be located on the ○th floor	The office is located on the 5th floor.	（事務室は 5 階に位置している）
~の中腹に位置する	be located halfway up	The village is located halfway up the mountain.	（村は山の中腹に位置している）

Activity Guide
Situation

周辺との関係

● 軸線に沿って	along the axis	Rooms are planned along the axis. (各室は軸線に沿って配置される)	
● ～へと視線が通る	have sight line toward	The floor plan has sight line toward the sea. (海への視線が通る平面計画)	
● 視線が行きかう	have multiple/ several lines of sight	People have multiple lines of sight on the bridge. (ブリッジで、人々の視線が行きかう)	
● ～を活かす	make use of		
地域特性を活かす	make use of local characteristics	a plan that makes use of local characteristics (地域特性を生かした計画)	
土地の風土を活かす	make use of regional features	a plan that makes use of regional features (土地の風土を活かした計画)	
地形を活かす	make use of natural landform	a section plan that makes use of natural landform (地形を活かした断面計画)	
● ～と調和する	harmonize with, match		
自然環境と調和する	harmonize with nature (/the natural environment)	a plan to harmonize with the natural environment (自然環境と調和した計画)	
周辺環境と調和する	harmonize with the surrounding environment	a color plan to harmonize with the surrounding environment (周辺環境と調和した色彩計画)	
地域景観と調和する	match the regional landscape	an elevation that matches the regional landscape (地域景観と調和した立面)	
● ～と連続する	consistent with, match		
周辺のスカイラインと連続する	consistent with the neighboring skyline	It's consistent with the neighboring skyline. (周辺のスカイラインと連続している)	

Activity Guide: Situation

	周辺環境と連続する	match the surrounding environment	The landscape matches the surrounding environment. (景色は周辺環境と連続している)
●	象徴的な意味	symbolic meaning	The site is situated at a place of symbolic meaning. (その敷地は象徴的な意味を持つ場所である)
●	記念碑的な意味	monumental significance	The gate was built at a site of monumental significance. (その門は記念碑的な意味を持つ場所に建てられた)
●	歴史的背景	historic background	The site has a historic background. (その敷地は歴史的背景を持つ場所である)
●	広がりのある	broad	This site offers a broad view of the landscape. (この場所には広大な景色がある)
●	アクセスのしやすさ	easy access	a design that offers easy access to the station (駅へアクセスしやすい計画)
●	〜のサーキュレーションを生む	design for ... to circulate	the plan designed for people to circulate around (人の流れのサーキュレーションを生む計画)
●	真南／真西／真東／真北を向く	face due south/west/east/north	The windows are facing due south. (真南を向いて窓がある)
●	〜に向かって	toward	toward the center of the city (街の中心部に向かって)
●	かっては〜だった	used to	This area used to be in ruins. (ここはかっては廃墟だった)

高低・勾配

●	高低差のある	difference in elevation	a site with a difference in elevation (高低差のある敷地)
●	高低差のない	no elevation	a site with no elevation (高低差のない敷地)
●	急勾配の	steep	a site in the middle of the steep hill (急勾配の丘の中腹に位置する敷地)

Activity Guide
Situation

● 緩勾配の	low-pitched	a site in the middle of a low-pitched hill （緩勾配の丘の中腹に位置する敷地）
● 緩やかにのぼる	go up gently	a slope that goes up gently （緩やかにのぼるスロープ）
● 緩やかにくだる	go down gently	a slope that goes down gently （緩やかにくだるスロープ）
● 上下をつなぐ	connect the top and bottom	a slope connecting the top and bottom （上下をつなぐスロープ）
● 斜面に沿う	stand on/go along a slope	The house stands on the slope. （その家は斜面に沿って建つ）
● 斜面に埋まった	under/embedded a slope	This room is under the slope. （この部屋は斜面に埋まっている）
● 斜面から突出する	extend out of/ protrude from a slope	The house extends out of the slope. （その家は斜面から突出して建つ）
● 等高線に沿う	follow contours	This plan follows the contours. （この計画は等高線に沿っている）

属性 （年齢層・世代／ライフスタイル・特性）

・・

年齢層・世代

● 20代の	in their twenties	The design concept of this car is targeted at those in their twenties. （この車のデザインコンセプトは20代をターゲットにしている）
● 乳児	baby, infant	This apartment is suitable for familes with babies. （このマンションは乳児がいる家庭向きだ）
● 子育て世代	families with small children	This house is suitable for families with small children. （この家は子育て世代向きだ）
● 団塊の世代	baby boomers	The design concept of this car is targeted at baby boomers. （この車のデザインコンセプトは団塊の世代をターゲットにしている）

Activity Guide
Situation

●	ベビーブーマー	baby boomers	This residential area is targeted at families of baby boomers. (この住宅地はベビーブーマー世代をターゲットにしている)
●	アクティブシニア	healthy and active senior citizens	This navigation system is targeted at healthy and active senior citizens. (このナビゲーションシステムはアクティブシニアをターゲットにしている)
●	高齢者	senior	This house is equipped with facilities for seniors. (この住宅は高齢者に向けた設備がある)
●	退職後の	after retirement	This residential area is good for people after retirement. (この住宅地は、退職後の人たちが住むのによい場所だ)

ライフスタイル・特性

●	～専用の	be intended for	This toy is intended for children over the age of ten. (この玩具は 10 歳以上の子ども専用だ)
		be reserved for	This apartment is reserved for female students only. (このマンションは女子学生専用です)
	女性専用の	for women only	The 9th floor of this hotel is for women only. (このホテルの 9 階は女性専用です)
	男性専用の	for men only	This dormitory is for men only. (この寄宿舎は男性専用です)
●	～を対象とした	be targeted at	This product is targeted at children who like puzzles. (この製品はパズル好きの子どもを対象としている)
●	～向きの	suitable for	Who is your product suitable for? (この製品はどんな人向けですか（誰が使いそうですか）)
●	好奇心旺盛な	with a lot of curiosity	The specifications of this navigation system will satisfy people with a lot of curiosity. (このナビゲーションシステムは好奇心旺盛な人でも満足できる仕様になっている)
●	～を趣味とする人	people who ... as a hobby	This navigation system is convenient for people who enjoy fishing as a hobby. (このナビゲーションシステムは釣りを趣味とする人にとって便利にできている)

Activity Guide
Situation

● 多趣味の人	people who have a lot of interests	This storage area is large enough for people who have a lot of interests. (この収納は多趣味の人にも十分な広さだ)
● 一人暮らしの人	people living alone	This apartment is targeted at young people living alone. (このマンションは一人暮らしの若者を対象にしている)
● 2人暮らしの夫婦	married couple without children	This house is suitable for married couples without children. (この家は2人暮らしの夫婦向けだ)
● 富裕層の	wealthy	The interior design of this shop should be targeted at the wealthy. (このショップのインテリアは富裕層をターゲットにしたデザインとする必要がある)
● 中間所得者層の	middle-income	This house is equipped for middle-income families. (この住宅は中間所得者層向けの設備がついている)
● 低所得者層の	low-income	This housing area was developed for low-income families. (この住宅地は低所得者層のために開発された)
● オフィスワーカー	office worker	The specifications of this watch are good for office workers. (この時計はオフィスワーカー向けの仕様になっている)
● 自宅で働く人	people working from home	This room layout is suitable for people working from home. (この間取りは自宅で働く人にとても適している)
● IT 好きの人	IT enthusiast	IT enthusiasts need a monitor they can use for long periods of time without getting tired. (IT 好きの人は長時間使っても疲れにくいモニターが必要だ)
● 働く主婦	working housewife	This kitchen tool will be extremely useful for working housewives. (このキッチンツールは働く主婦を大いに助けるだろう)
● 熟練者	expert	This DIY kit is intended for experts. (この DIY キットは熟練者専用の仕様です)
● 初心者	amateur	These prosumer cameras are also targeted at amateurs. (このセミプロ向けのカメラは初心者も対象としている)
● オタク	geek, nerd	Computer geeks often get excited by new technology. (コンピューターオタクはしばしば、新しい技術に興奮する)
● ヘビーユーザー	heavy user	He is a heavy user of these products. (彼はその製品のヘビーユーザーだ)

Activity Guide: Situation

- 流行に敏感な　　　trendy　　　　　　　　The features of this chair will satisfy trendy people.
　　　　　　　　　　　　　　　　　　　　　（この椅子のディテールなら流行に敏感な人も満足するだろう）

- 障害のある　　　　with a disability,　　　This house is accessible for family members with disabilities.
　　　　　　　　　　physically　　　　　　（この家は障害のある方がいる家庭向きです）
　　　　　　　　　　challenged

Activity Guide
Light and Shadow

状況・状態

● 発光する	phosphorescent	Using phosphorescent materials makes it safer. （発光する素材を使うことでより安全になる）	
● ぴかっと光る	flashing	Using a flashing sign draws attention and gives warning. （ぴかっと光るサインを使って注意喚起する）	
● 点滅する	blinking, flickering	Have a blinking light function to warn of danger. （危険を知らせるために点滅機能をつけなさい）	
● 漏れる光	light filtering in	Moderate the amount of light filtering in to create a sense of distance. （光の漏れる量を調節し距離感を演出しなさい）	
● キラキラする	glitter, sparkle	The metallic flecks in the paint glitter in the light. （塗料のメタリックの粒に光が当たるとキラキラする）	
● ぼんやりとした光	dull light	Use dull light so that it doesn't become a hindrance. （ぼんやりとした光を使うことで、邪魔にならないようにしなさい）	
● 自然光のもとで	in natural light	a dressing room that allows users to see how their clothes look in natural light （自然光のもとで服の見え方が確認できる試着室）	
● 照明のもとで	under the light	I can't see it properly. Can you put it under the light? （よく見えません。照明のもとに置いていただけますか）	
● 拡散した光	diffused light	The diffused light brings a feeling of contentment. （拡散した光が安らぎをもたらす）	
● 反射させた	reflected	Please enjoy the effects of the reflected light. （反射光の効果を楽しんでください）	
● 柔らかい光に満ちた	full of soft light	I chose the south-facing room which is full of soft light. （柔らかい光に満ちた南向きの部屋を選んだ）	
● 鋭い光が差し込む	be penetrated by sharp light	a sunroom that is penetrated by sharp light （鋭い光が差し込んだサンルーム）	
● 強い影	dark shadows	Create an atmosphere in the interior by using a light source that casts dark shadows. （強い影を落とす光源を使ってインテリアに特徴を創りなさい）	

Activity Guide
Light and Shadow

● 繊細な影	delicate shade	Please hang out under the delicate shade of a tree. (繊細な影を落とす木陰でくつろいでください)
● 降り注ぐ光	light pouring in	Create a meditative space through the construction of light pouring in over time. (時間と共に光が降り注ぐ瞑想空間を設計しなさい)
● 陰影のある	shaded	Create variation in a dull space with a shaded wall surface. (陰影のある壁面で退屈な空間に変化を与えなさい)
● ほのかな明かり	faint light, dim	I want to create an atmosphere using faint light. (ほのかに明るい照明効果で雰囲気をつくりたい)

行為

● 間接照明でほのかに照らす	use indirect illumination, faintly lighted	Create a relaxed environment by using indirect illumination. (間接照明でリラックスした環境を演出しなさい)
● 調光する	adjust/modulate the light	You can adjust the light in the room to fit the mood. (雰囲気に合わせて部屋の照明を調光できる)
● 明るさを制御する	control brightness	The position and size of the toplight control the brightness. (トップライトの位置と大きさで明るさを制御する)
● 光（日差し）を導き入れる（取り入れる）	allow the sunlight in	Opening the shutters in the morning allows the sunlight in. (朝のうちにシャッターを開けて日差しを取り入れる)
● 光を和らげる	soften the light	By softening the light, it creates a more efficient living space. (光を和らげることで効果的な住空間をつくる)
● 光をさえぎる	block the light, protect light	The trees block the sunlight, creating a comfortable environment. (木々が太陽の光をさえぎってほどよい状況をつくる)
● 照明を足す	add illumination	Accentuate the living space by adding illumination. (照明を足すことで部屋にアクセントをつけなさい)
● 美しい影を落とす	cast a beautiful shade	Use lighting equipment that casts a beautiful shade. (美しい影を落とす照明器具を使いなさい)
● 暗くする、減光する	dim the light	Dimming the light will create a relaxing mood. (暗くすることでリラックスした雰囲気になる)

Activity Guide
Light and Shadow

その他

● 光源	light source	Make use of the available light source for each room. (それぞれの部屋に合った光源を選びなさい)
● 蓄光	glow-in-the-dark	Use glow-in-the-dark materials to more clearly see the steps on the stairs. (階段のステップが視認できるように蓄光素材を使いなさい)
● 蛍光塗料	flourescent paint	This sign stands out because of the flourescent paint. (この表示は蛍光塗料で目立っている)
● 木漏れ日	sunlight filtering through the trees	The sunlight filtering through the trees creates a sense of space. (木漏れ日が空間を演出する)
● 反射した光	reflected light	Create a distinctive atmosphere through the use of reflected light. (反射した光で特徴のある雰囲気をつくりなさい)
● 遮光	light shielding, shade	A window that provides sufficient light shielding should be included in the design. (遮光性能を備えた窓をとり入れた設計が求められる)
● 陰となる面	shadow-covered surface	Control the colors of the shadow-covered surface. (陰となる面の色調をコントロールしなさい)
● 光の当たる面	where the light strikes	The color looks different depending on where the light strikes it. (光の当たる面によって色が違って見える)
● 透過した光	light through	The soft light through the sliding paper doors is beautiful. (障子を透過した柔らかい光が美しい)
● 強い光	strong light	Strong and weak light are used separately. (強い光と弱い光が使い分けられている)
● 細かい光	fine light	The sparkling effect of fine light adds a characteristic accent on it. (細かい光のキラキラが特徴的なアクセントとなっている)
● 光のコントラスト	contrast	Improve stair safety by emphasizing the contrast. (光のコントラストを強調し階段の安全性を向上させなさい)
● 明るい場所	a brightly lit place	Putting the product in a brightly lit place makes its flaws easy to notice. (明るい場所に製品を置くと欠点が目立ちやすくなる)
● うす暗い場所	a dimly lit place	A dimly lit place is suitable for meditation. (暗い場所は瞑想にふさわしい)

Activity Guide
Function

状況・状態

●	伸びる	lengthen	The table can be lengthened to adapt to the number of people. (そのテーブルは多人数に対応するために拡張できる)
●	(変な)音が出る	make a strange sound/noise	Recently, my car has been making a strange sound. (最近、車から変な音が出る)
●	(良い)音が出る	produce (good) sound	Our new speakers produce high-quality sound. (新しいスピーカーは高質な音を出す)
●	音の良い定位	good sound orientation	The hall has fairly good sound orientation. (そのホールの音の定位はとても良い)
●	コンパクトになる	become compact	This foldable bicycle can become compact, making it suitable for storage and portability. (この折りたたみ自転車は、コンパクトになることで収納と持ち運びに適している)
●	折りたたみ収納式の	foldaway	The glovebox comes with a foldaway tray. (グローブボックスには折りたたみ収納式のトレイがある)
●	静音性の高い	quiet, less noise	This vacuum cleaner is very quiet while offering the same level of functionality. (この掃除機は同性能の中では静音性が高い)
●	制震(機能)	vibration control	a drum-type washing machine with vibration control (制震機能のあるドラム式洗濯機)
●	AとBを兼ねる	combine A and B	By combining A and B, we will be able to reduce costs. (AとBを兼ねることでコストを下げることができる)
●	収納可能な	storable	Extra parts for the vacuum cleaner are easily storable. (掃除機の付属部品は簡単に収納可能だ)
●	機能に応じて	according to the function	Each box is used according to its function. (それぞれの箱は機能に応じて利用されている)
●	使いやすさ	ease of use	Outstanding ease of use! (抜群の使いやすさだ)

Activity Guide
Function

行為

● 早く暖める	heat quickly	Although this small electric fan-heater doesn't have the power to heat a whole room, it can heat up a small area quickly. (この小型電気ファンヒーターは部屋全体を暖める力はないが、部分的に早く暖めることができる)	
● ～に風を送る	fan	Fan and strengthen the fire. (風を送って火を強くしなさい)	
● 開閉する	open and close	Use a magnetic catch to reduce the stress when it opens and closes. (開閉時のストレスを軽減させるマグネットキャッチを使いなさい)	
● 昇降する	lift	I am using this truck with a lift function to move. (昇降する機能を備えたトラックで引っ越しする)	
● 伸縮自在の	elastic	The elastic material prevents slipping. (伸縮する機能を持った素材がスリップを防ぐ)	
● ～を巻き取る	wind	Ensure the safety and appearance by using a winding cord. (コードを巻き取ることで安全性と見た目を確保しなさい)	
● 吸引する	vacuum	For a recharger, this vacuums powerfully. (充電式にしては力強く吸引する)	
● ～を吸着する	absorb	Dust is absorbed by static electricity. (静電気でホコリを吸着させる)	
● ～を抽出する	brew, extract, distill	Brew (up) coffee. (コーヒーを淹れなさい)	
● ～を誘引する	induce	sleep-inducing music (眠気を誘引する音楽)	
● ～を誘発する	encourage	It encourages people to operate it intuitively. (それは自然に操作を誘発する)	
● ～を誘発する(ソフトウェア内で)	prompt	This software program prompts the user to input their data of birth. (そのソフトウェアプログラムはユーザーに出生データを入力するように促す)	
● 案内する	guide	a system that guides drivers to the destination (ドライバーを目的地に案内するシステム)	

Activity Guide
Function

● ～を支援する	assist	a service that assists new users （初心者を支援するサービス）
● ～を選別する	distinguish, sort	a tray that can easily distinguish different coins （簡単にコインを選別することができるトレイ）
● ～を照らす	light up	The motion sensor activates a security floorlight which lights up the garden at night. （モーションセンサーが夜に庭を照らすフロアライトを作動させる）
● ～を表示する	show, express	Show that the operating procedures are easy to understand. （操作手順を分かりやすく表示しなさい）
● ～を投影する	image	The doctor imaged the cell on the slide. （博士はその細胞をスライド上に投影した）
● ～を投影する	project	It is fashionable to project interactive computer graphics on public buildings. （建物へのコンピューターグラフィックスの投影が流行している）
● ～を切り替える（調整する）	modify	The function can be modified by changing attachments. （アタッチメントの交換で機能の切り替えが可能となる）
● 冷却する	cool	High performance can be maintained by the ability to cool. （冷却することによって高性能を保つことができる）
● 冷凍する	freeze	The freezing compartment has a flash freeze function to keep food fresh. （その冷凍庫は食品鮮度を保つ瞬間冷凍機能を備えている）
● 加熱する	heat	The heating conditions are easy to see, which prevents burns. （加熱状態が分かりやすいのでやけど防止になっている）
● ～を蒸す	steam	Steaming is a technique often used in home cooking. （蒸すことは家庭料理の中でよく使われる手法だ）
● ～を焼く	grill, bake, roast	Expert grilling comes down to how well you apply heat. （上手に焼くコツは火加減による）
● ～を除湿する	dehumidify	It has a dehumidifying function to keep the room comfortable. （部屋を快適にするための除湿機能を備えている）
● ～を乾燥させる	dry	Air conditioners dry the air in the room. （エアコンで部屋の空気を乾燥させる）
● ～を乾燥させる（脱水する）	dehydrate	This machine dehydrates vegetables to preserve them. （この機械は野菜を保存するために乾燥させる）

Activity Guide
Function

● 〜を洗浄する	clean, cleanse	It has a cleaning function built-in so it always stays clean. （自ら洗浄する機能が付いているのでいつまでも清潔だ）
● 〜を包む	wrap	Books are better protected when shrink-wrapped. （書籍はシュリンク包装の方が保護される）
● 〜を覆う	cover	Cover it to keep it from gathering dust. （ホコリを避けるために覆いなさい）
● 〜にふたをする	put a lid on	Putting a lid on it protects against humidity. （ふたをすることで湿気から守る）
● 閉まる	close	The rear door closes automatically when this button is pushed. （ボタンを押すと後方ドアが自動的に閉まる）
● 〜を集める	collect	It can easily collect and get rid of even fine dust. （細かなチリも簡単に集めて捨てることができる）
● 〜を捨てる	throw away	PET bottles can be recylced and reused rather than thrown away. （ペットボトルは捨てずに再生利用することができる）
● 〜を拾う	pick up	Please pick me up in front of the station. （駅前で私を拾ってください）
● 〜を取りはずす	remove (removable)	a storage pocket that is removable when necessary （必要に応じて取りはずすことができる収納ポケット）
● 収納する	store	Store the tools in the box. （箱に道具をしまいなさい）
● 〜を繋ぐ	connect	Your smartphone and car can be connected via Bluetooth. （スマートフォンと車をブルートゥースで繋ぐことができる）
● AとBを分ける	separate A and B	That machine separates the light parts and heavy parts. （そのマシーンは軽いパーツと重いパーツを分ける）
● AとBを緩やかに繋ぐ	loosely connect A and B	We need to consider a way that A and B can be loosely connected. （AとBを緩やかに繋ぐ方法を検討する必要がある）
● 〜を和らげる	soften, moderate	It's important to have a seat that softens vibrations caused by driving over road surfaces. （路面からの振動を和らげるシートが必要だ）
● 〜を強調する	emphasize	Devise a plan that emphasizes strength. （堅牢性を強調するための工夫をしなさい）
● 〜を増幅させる	amplify	We are developing an amplifying apparatus. （増幅させる装置を開発している）

Activity Guide
Function

- ～を折りたたむ　　fold, diffract　　The antenna can be folded to prevent accidents.
（事故防止のためにアンテナを折りたたむことができる）

～性

- 安全性、危険性　　safety, risk　　After confirming safety, we can proceed to the next step.
（安全性を確保した上で次のステップに進む）

- 耐久性　　durability　　Customers demand a product that has durability and is cost-effective.
（顧客は耐久性があり、価格に見合った製品を求める）

- 耐熱性　　heat resistance　　Consider how to increase heat resistance.
（耐熱性を高める方法を検討しなさい）

- 耐寒性　　cold resistance　　We need to purchase a device that can measure cold resistance.
（耐寒性をテストする装置を購入する必要がある）

- 耐候性　　weather resistance　　Weather resistance testing is an indespensible part of product development.
（耐候性の実験は製品開発に欠かせない項目だ）

- 耐食性　　corrosion resistance　　I am going to cover my house with a corrosion resistant roof.
（耐食性の高い屋根で覆うつもりだ）

- 退色性　　color fastness　　Color fastness is something we need to keep in mind.
（退色性に配慮した色使いを心がける）

- 視認性、可読性　　readability, visibility　　Readability is a priority.
（視認性の高い表示を心がける）

- 透過性　　permeability　　Put together materials with high permeability.
（透過性を追求した材料を組み立てなさい）

- 親和性　　affinity　　Use the best color scheme to increase the product's user-affinity.
（製品の親和性を高めるために最もよい色彩を使いなさい）

- 走破性　　drivability　　Design in a way that improves drivability.
（走破性を向上させる設計にしなさい）

- 操作性　　operability　　Operability is good even during high-speed driving.
（高速走行中でさえも操作性が良い）

- 乗降性　　getting on and off　　Getting on and off is easy even for the elderly.
（高齢者でも乗降性が良い）

Activity Guide
Application

Applications

● ~に応募する	apply for		Please download the attached document if you want to apply for the contest. (コンテストに応募を希望する場合は添付書類をダウンロードしてください)
● ~に記入する	fill in		Please fill in the application completely before you send it. (応募書類は送る前に全て記入してください)
● 未完成	incomplete		Your application is incomplete. You need your signature at the bottom. (応募書類が未完成です。下部に署名をしてください)
● ~を受け入れる、採用する	accept		Congratulations! Your design has been accepted into the competition! (おめでとうございます。本コンペにてあなたのデザインが採用となりました)
● ~を却下する(拒否する)	reject		I applied for the competition but unfortunately I was rejected. (コンペに応募したが残念ながら採用されなかった)
● ~を参照する	refer to		Please refer to the attached document for an explanation of how to fill out the application. (添付された応募書類記入の説明書類を参照してください)
● ~に馴れる、習熟する	familiarize oneself with		Please familiarize yourself with the guidelines before completing the application. (応募書類を完成させる前にガイドラインをよく理解しておいてください)
● 締め切り	deadline		The deadline for submission is August 29th. (提出の締め切りは8月29日です)
● ~を提出する	submit		Please submit your application by the end of next week. (来週末までに応募用紙を提出してください)

Competitions

● 資格のない	ineligible		Anyone over the age of 30 is ineligible for the competition. (30歳以上の方はコンペに応募できません)

214

Activity Guide
Application

● ～の資格を有する	qualify for	The winner will qualify for the solo show at the gallery. (優勝者はそのギャラリーで個展を開く資格を得られる)
● 資格がない、剥奪されている	disqualified	He was disqualified because he submitted his product in another competition. (彼はその作品を他のコンペに提出していたので応募資格がなかった)
● 授与	award	Mika received an award for most promising design. (ミカはもっとも有望なデザインとして賞を受賞した)
● ガイドライン	guidelines	For more information about the competition, please refer to the guidelines. (本コンペの詳細情報は、ガイドラインを参照してください)
● 規定	rules and regulations	The rules and regulations for the competition are included in the attached PDF. (コンペに関する規定は、添付のPDFに記載されています)
● よくある質問	FAQ	If you have any questions, please refer to the following FAQ. (質問のある方は、以下の「よくある質問」を参照してください)
● 提案	proposal	I read your proposal and I think it has a strong chance of being accepted. (あなたの提案を見ましたが採用の可能性が高いと思います)
● 企画	project	She has worked on several projects, both personally and professionally. (彼女は公私含め、数々の企画に参加してきた)
● 登録	registration	Registration for the competition must be completed by the end of the week. (コンペへの登録は週末までに完了しなくてはならない)
● 審査	screening	Results for the initial screening will be announced on Tuesday. (一次審査の結果は火曜日に通知される)
● 消印を押された	postmarked	Your application must be postmarked on or before June 25th. (応募は6月25日までの消印有効です)
● 郵便	post	Please submit your application by post. (応募は郵便でお願いします)

Activity Guide
Application

Biographies

● 1年生、2年生、3年生、4年生	freshman, sophmore, junior, senior	Taro is currently a junior at Temple University. （タロウはテンプル大学の3年生である）
● 業績（達成）	achievement, accomplishment	One of Mika's many achievements was winning the Fields Medal in 2012. （2012年のフィールドメダルは、ミカの多くの業績のうちの1つだ）
● 特徴	attributes, characteristics	Peter has several strong attributes such as creativity and attention to detail. （ペーターの特徴は創造性と細部へのこだわりだ）
● 強い影響がある	influential	Alex has been very influential in the world of graphic design. （アレックスは世界のグラフィックデザインに大きな影響を及ぼしている）
● 影響	impact	His works have had a strong impact in her area of design. （彼の作品は彼女のデザイン領域に大きな衝撃を与えた）
● 視点	perspective	She brings a unique perspective to the area of product design. （彼女は製品デザインの分野にユニークな視点をもたらしている）
● 貢献	contribution	Hiroki has made a strong contribution to the development of CG and Art. （ヒロキはＣＧアートの発展に大きな貢献をした）
● 野心	ambition	It is his strong ambition to combine creativity and innovation in his work. （創造と改革の融合は彼の大きな野望だ）

● 著者プロフィール

高山 靖子
静岡文化芸術大学デザイン学部デザイン学科（プロダクト領域）教授。博士（芸術工学）。愛知県立芸術大学美術学部卒業。株式会社東芝を経て現職。

亀井 暁子
静岡文化芸術大学デザイン学部デザイン学科（建築・環境領域）准教授。一級建築士。京都大学大学院工学研究科建築学専攻修了。株式会社日本設計を経て現職。

高瀬 奈美
静岡文化芸術大学英語中国語教育センター特任講師。コロンビア大学ティーチャーズカレッジ卒業。英語教授法修士課程修了。

服部 守悦
静岡文化芸術大学デザイン学部デザイン学科（プロダクト領域）准教授。武蔵野美術大学造形学部卒業。スズキ株式会社を経て現職。

峯 郁郎
静岡文化芸術大学デザイン学部デザイン学科（プロダクト領域）教授。愛知県立芸術大学美術学部卒業。ヤマハ株式会社を経て現職。

Edward Sarich
静岡文化芸術大学文化政策学部国際文化学科准教授。バーミンガム大学応用言語学修士課程修了。静岡大学非常勤講師を経て現職。

Gary McLeod
写真研究家。博士（写真）。ロンドン芸術大学ロンドン・カレッジ・オブ・コミュニケーション・メディア学部卒業。トルコ・イズミル経済大学美術・デザイン学部講師を経て現職。

Jack Ryan
静岡文化芸術大学文化政策学部国際文化学科准教授。米国テンプル大学教育学修士課程修了。愛知大学豊橋校講師を経て現職。

Mark Sheehan
阪南大学国際コミュニケーション学部教授。米国マサチューセッツ州立大学英文学修士課程修了。静岡文化芸術大学准教授を経て現職。

著作権法上、無断複写・複製は禁じられています。

DESIGN ENGLISH — クリエイターのための闘う英語

2016 年 8 月 19 日　　　1 刷

著　者 —	高山 靖子	Yasuko Takayama
	亀井 暁子	Akiko Kamei
	高瀬 奈美	Nami Takase
	服部 守悦	Moriyoshi Hattori
	峯 郁郎	Ikuro Mine
	サリッチ・エドワード	Edward Sarich
	マクラウド・ギャリー	Gary McLeod
	ライアン・ジャック	Jack Ryan
	シーハン・マーク	Mark Sheehan
発行者	南雲 一範	
発行所 —	株式会社　南雲堂	

〒162-0801　東京都新宿区山吹町 361
TEL　03-3268-2311（営業部）
TEL　03-3268-2387（編集部）
FAX　03-3269-2486（営業部）
振替　00160-0-4686

組版／Office haru　　　装丁／銀月堂
印刷所／日本ハイコム株式会社　　製本所／松村製本所

Printed in Japan　　乱丁・落丁本はお取り替えいたします。＜検印省略＞
ISBN 978-4-523-26543-6　　C0082　　　　[1-543]

E-mail　nanundo@post.email.ne.jp
URL　　http://www.nanun-do.co.jp

DESIGN ENGLISH
― クリエイターのための闘う英語 ―

Sample Dialogue 和訳

Activities 解答例

南雲堂

Unit 1
Color

Dialogue 1　文字と背景色

A: 赤と緑の**対比**でロゴを**目立たせる**のはいいけど、ハレーションが起きて見づらくなるね。
B: 少し**彩度**を落としてなじませ**てはどうかな**？
A: グラデーションをつけるという手もあるね。
B: でも、ロゴと背景の面積比のバランスも考慮すべきだよね。
A: こちら側は、白にグレーの落ち着いた雰囲気にしようとしているけど、ロゴが目立たないね。
B: ロゴの**明度**を下げて、もっとコントラストを強めては**どう**？

．．．

Q1: AとBは、何を提案していますか？
They are suggesting ways to improve the logo by adjusting the saturation or gradation.
（彼らは、彩度やグラデーションを調整してロゴを改善する方法を提案しています。）

Q2: あなたならロゴを改善するために何を提案しますか？
(e.g.) What about using white for the background and highly saturated red for the logo with a drop shadow?
（背景を白にしてロゴに彩度の高い赤を使って影をつけてはどうでしょうか？）

Unit 1
Color

Dialogue 2　色の統一感

A: サイン計画では色に**統一感**を出すことが重要だけれど、警告を意味するものには**注意をひく**黄色を使いたいね。
B: 背景色にコーポレートカラーの紺色を使っ**てはどうかな**？
A: **なるほど**。そうすれば、全体のイメージを統一できるし、**視認性**も高まるね。
B: 書体は何にしようか？
A: 少し離れていても**可読性の高い**種類を使おう。

....

Q1: 彼らはなぜ黄色と紺色を使用しているのですか？
They are using yellow and navy blue because it keeps the unity of the colors and also emphasizes the warning signs.
（彼らが黄色と紺を使っているのは、色の統一感を持たせるだけでなく、警告の標識を強調するためです。）

Q2: あなたなら他にどんな色を使用しますか？それはなぜですか？
　　(e.g.) How about using dark green in the background, which would be a little warmer?
　　　　（背景に濃い緑を使ってもう少し温かみを出したらどうでしょうか？）

Unit 1
Color

Dialogue 3　中庭の色彩構成

A: コンクリートのグレーが多くて、支配的だね。無彩色でまとめる**色彩計画**だったのかな。
B: **色味を足す**といい**と思わない**？
A: そう言われてみると、緑が、面積は小さいが**全体を引締めて**いるね。
B: キャンパスカラーをサインに使って、**アクセントをつける**こともできるね。

....

Q: 彼らは、その色彩構成を向上させるために何を提案していますか？
They are suggesting that adding a little shade would make it better.
（少し色味を足すともっと良くなると提案しています。）

Unit 1
Color

Dialogue 4 ボディーカラーの検討

A: この車は、塗る色によって全く違った見え方をするね。
B: キャラクターカラーは、新しい**光輝材**を使って元気が出る色にしたんだ。**逆に**ギラギラ感(**ギラギラする**感じ)のない色を、街に馴染む落ち着いたベーシックカラーのラインナップとしたんだ。
A: どの色も表情があるし、材料着色の部分とも上手くマッチしているね。

....

Q1: キャラクター(コミュニケーション)カラーにキラキラした素材を使うことについて、あなたはどう思いますか?ベーシックカラーを使う場合と何が異なると思いますか?
   (e.g.) Using shiny materials with communication colors make them look vibrant, unlike basic colors, which project a calm feeling.
   (落ちついた表情を持つベーシックな色と違って、光輝材を使ったキャラクターカラーは元気な感じがします。)

Q2: あなたはどんな色や素材をこの車に使用しますか?
   (e.g.) I would use basic colors because they are more affordable.
   (私は価格が手頃だからベーシックな色を使います。)

Unit 1
Color

Dialogue 5　工房の**色彩計画**

A: 濃い木質系の色が出ると重くなりがちだけど、全体をグレー系（の色彩）でまとめているからクールな印象だね？
B: 露出した空調ダクトも、天井の色と馴染む色遣いだよね？
A: インテリア全体を、落ち着いた色遣いにしているから、創作意欲が湧くよ。創造の場所らしい色彩を意識した**のかな**？

....

Q: 写真の部屋の色彩計画は何を意図していると思いますか？
　(e.g.) For me, the color scheme projecting from the room makes me think about honesty and hard work.
　（この部屋の色彩計画のおかげで、一生懸命仕事に取り組むことができると思います。）
　(e.g.) I think that this color scheme is aiming to have students to concentrate on their creation by avoiding using any highly saturated colors.
　（この色彩計画は、彩度の高い色を使わないことで、学生が創作に集中できるようにしていると思います。）
　(e.g.) I think the neutral color scheme was intended for students to be able to concentrate on their work objectively without any irrelevant influences.
　（無彩色の色彩計画によって、学生が気を散らさず、作業に集中できるようにしたと思います。）

Unit 2
Form

Dialogue 1　ドライヤーのモックアップ

A: 全体的にシンプルでよくまとまった形だね。
B: そうだね。特に、風の吹き出し口に向かって**細くなった**ラインが優美できれいだね。
A: **欲を言えば**、持ち手の形をもっと握りやすくできないかな？
B: 形は変えたくないから、**でこぼこ**をつけてはどう？
A: すっきりとした形が台無しだよ。

....

Q: 彼らは何の変更について話していますか？
　 They are talking about possible changes to the handle to make it easier to grip.
　（彼らは、握りやすくするためにハンドルの変更点について話しています。）

Unit 2
Form

Dialogue 2   ユニークな椅子

A: 二本足にすることで軽快なデザインになったね。
B: 足に**テーパー**をつけて、さらに軽さを出しました。
A: 強度は大丈夫なの？座ったときの安定感はどう？
B: はい、大丈夫です。脚部は途中にブリッジを渡して強化していますし、お尻を支える部分は厚くしてあります。でも、形のイメージが重くなりがちなので、ボリュームのある部分をシャープなハイライトエッジで引き締め**てみました**。

....

Q: この椅子の特徴は何ですか？
The legs are tapered to take up less space and to create a sense of lightness, but also strength.
（テーパーを使ってボリューム感を減らし、軽快さを感じさせながら強度も出しています。）

Unit 2
Form

Dialogue 3　テーブルデザインの工夫

A: テーパーのついた形で軽快なテーブルになったね。
B: 薄いトレイが出て来るのも楽しい表情になっているでしょう？
A: でも、特にトレイを出したときに不安定な印象があるんだけど。
B: 台座の端面だけ、**逆テーパー**に加工することで少しでも安定するように工夫はしました。
A: **一見**4枚の板が浮いているように見えるね。
B: はい、浮遊感と軽快さを表現したかったのです。

....

Q: あなたは、このテーブルのどこが好きですか？またどこが嫌いですか？その理由は？
　(e.g.) I like that the four layers are functional as well as aesthetically pleasing. You can put things like shelves on them. However, I don't like the trays because they disrupt the clean form.
　（私は、4枚のレイヤーが美しいだけでなく機能的なところが好きです。棚のように物を置けます。しかし、私はきれいなフォームを邪魔するトレイは好きではありません。）

Unit 2
Form

Dialogue 4　新しいパッケージ方法

A:「靴のパッケージは箱である」という先入観を取り払っていて、新鮮だね。

B: どのサイズにも使える、くるっと巻いて包む方法を思いついたんです。

A: 靴底が見えていることで中身がすぐ分かって、省力化と機能との両立が成功していると思う。

B: さらに、フレキシブルなパッケージは靴の形になじみます。

A: スタッキングにも対応できていて、シンプルな形で楽しさを表現しているから、カジュアルな子ども用シューズのパッケージに最適だね。

・・・

Q: このパッケージを使うメリットは何ですか？

This package has several advantages. First, they can be used to wrap shoes of any size. Second, we can see the soles of the shoes without opening the box. Third, they can be stacked easily.

（このパッケージには、いくつかの利点があります。はじめにどんなサイズの靴でも包むことができます。二つ目は、靴のソール部分を箱を開けなくても見ることができます。三つ目は、簡単に積めることです。）

Unit 2
Form

Dialogue 5　カーブによる効果

A: 低層部の屋根は**緩やかな曲線**で**滑らかにうねり**、柔らかい印象をつくり出しているね。
B: そのうねりは、室内の形状などに利用されているの？
A: 室内の天井がアールをつけた形状になっているし、屋上は、ふっくらと波打つ緑の丘となっているよ。
B: **傾斜した**空中庭園に立つと、不思議な感覚になるだろうね。

....

Q: 屋根にはどんな特徴がありますか？
　　The low-rise section of the roof has a gentle curve with a smooth undulation that gives an impression of suppleness, and it creates the mysterious feeling of standing in a sloping garden in the sky.
　　（低層部の屋根は緩やかな曲線で滑らかにうねり、柔らかい印象をつくり出しています。そして空中で傾斜した庭園に立っているような不思議な感覚を生みます。）

Unit 2
Form

Dialogue 6　外壁の特徴

A: ほとんどの高層ビルは凹凸のない形で**威圧的**に見えるけど、この建物ではそれを変えたかったんだ。
B: 具体的には、何を**試み**たの？
A: **スリットを入れて2つのボリュームに分け**て、外壁やバルコニーはぎざぎざした突出のある形状としたよ。
B: 外壁の凹凸は、細かい襞のようだね。
A: 外壁をわずかに斜めに傾けることによって、他の建物と視線をずらす効果もあるよ。

....

Q: 外壁の特徴を説明しましょう。
The outer wall may appear uneven but it is designed to shift your line of sight off of other buildings.
（外側の壁は不揃いのように見えますが、他の建物から視線をそらすようにデザインされています。）

Unit 2
Form

Dialogue 7　モデルの造形

A: 基本的には、**断面**が強く、塊感があるね。
B: うん、だけど**面構成**の辻褄が合ってないところがある。
A: 顔周りだけど、要素が多くてうるさいから、もっとすっきりさせた方がいいと思うけど。
B: **それはどうかな**。最近はもっとゴツくした方がウケるよ。
A: わかった。**好きにしなよ**。

....

Q: Aは何を提案していますか？
A is suggesting that B reduce the number of elements around the face to make it less busy.
（Aは、顔周りがごちゃごちゃしないようにBに要素を減らすように提案しています。）

Unit 2
Form

Dialogue 8　車内の開放感

A: インストゥルメントパネルは、<u>圧迫感</u>があるように見えるね。
B: そうかなぁ、これぐらい厚い方が安心感があると思うけど……。
A: いや、もっと開放感を出す必要があるよ。
B: じゃあ、修正案を考えてみるよ。

....

Q: あなたなら B にどんな助言をしますか?
　(e.g.) You should shave a bit off the top to make it look like it has less volume.
　　(ボリュームを減らすために、上面を少し削った方がいいです。)

Unit 3
Material

Dialogue 1　特性と用途

A: 本体はプラスチック素材だけど、吸気口周りはクローム**メッキ加工**にしたいんです。
B: そうすると全体に冷たい印象だね。別の素材を使ってもう少し温かみのある素材感が出せないかな？木材とか？
A: 燃えちゃいますよ。それよりクールな風をイメージして、**光沢のある**素材や**透明感のある**素材が使いたかったんです。
B: 持ち手はどうする？つるつるしていたら滑るじゃないか。
A: シボ加工などの表面処理ですべり止めに対応したいと考えています。

. . . .

Q: 他にどのような素材が本体や持ち手に使えるでしょうか？
　　(e.g.) I would like to use silicone rubber for the grip surface and acrylic resin for the body.
　　（私はグリップにシリコンゴムを、本体にはアクリル樹脂を使いたいと思います。）

Unit 3
Material

Dialogue 2　適性と可能性

A: 脚は**アルミのダイキャスト**にするの？
B: **今、悩んでいるところです**。できるだけ軽くしたいので、チタンとかカーボンも検討しました。
A: コストが高くなりすぎないかな？それより、座面の素材は何？
B: ABS樹脂の**ブロー成形で**、塗装仕上げを考えています。
A: お尻が痛そうだけど、シリコンとかの柔らかい素材を使うとか、**布を巻く**とかしないの？
B: **野暮ったくないですか？**

....

Q: あなたなら、脚と座面にどのような素材を使いますか？
(e.g.) I think iron would be best for the legs and a polyurethane form covered with leather for the seat.
（私は、椅子の脚には鉄で、座面には革で覆われたポリウレタンが良いと思います。）

Unit 3
Material

Dialogue 3　素材選択とコスト配分

A: 集成材を使ったカジュアルな木製家具の提案だね。
B: **無垢材**に比べるとコストがかなり下がります。
A: 板と板との間隔を保つ柱部分には**アクリル**を使ったんだね？
B: はい、板以外の部分はできるだけ存在感を弱めたいと思って、**透明**で丈夫な素材を使いました。
A: アクリルは比較的高価だけど？
B: 大部分に安価な集成材を使用したので、全体の**コスト**は適正になっていると思います。

．．．

Q: 柱部分にアクリルを使うことで、他にどのような長所、短所がありますか？
Acrylic is durable and transparent so it can express a light and floating image. However, it is also expensive.
（アクリルは丈夫で、しかも透明なので軽さや浮遊感を出すことができます。しかし値段が高いです。）

Unit 3
Material

Dialogue 4　素材選択と利点

A: 柔らかくて子どもの靴のさまざまなサイズや形に合わせられるので、包装には**段ボール**を使用しました。

B: それはいいアイデアだね。強くて**表情のある**素材だものね。靴ってたいてい**ボール紙**の四角い箱に入っているけど、このパッケージを使えば高品質に見えるよ。

A: ありがとうございます。さらに言えば、平面だけど包める素材のおかげで、全体的に軽い印象になると思うんです。

....

Q: このデザインはボール紙の四角い箱よりどのように優れているでしょうか？

This design is better than a rectangular cardboard box because it can be folded to fit different sizes and shapes, it gives the impression of a high quality product. It is strong yet expressive, and has a light feeling.

（このデザインの方がボール紙の四角い箱より優れた点があります。それはいろいろなサイズや形に合わせられること、より質の高い印象を与えること、強度もあるけれど表情もあって、軽快な雰囲気にもなっていることです。）

Unit 3
Material

Dialogue 5　建物の素材検討

A: 架構はコンクリート打ち放し、外壁はリブ形状のセメント板をはめ込んだ仕上げだね。
B: リブは、工業製品らしい、繊細で規則正しい表情だね。
A: **他にも**、シルバーのアルミ庇や、**亜鉛メッキ仕上げ**の手すりなどは、風合いと素材を生かした組み合わせだね。
B: きっと、耐久性にも配慮したのだろうね。

．．．

Q: この建物にはどのような素材が使われているか説明してください。
Ribbed cement paneling was used for the outer wall and aluminum paneling was used for the canopy.
（外壁には、リブ形状のセメント板が使われています。庇には、アルミニウムパネルが使われています。）

Unit 3
Material

Dialogue 6　インテリア素材の検討

A: 講堂のインテリアは、「ボードに**塗装**」と、木製パネルの組み合わせで、落ち着いていて温かみのある印象だね。
B: 木の壁は、目地を活かしたデザインにしているのかな？
A: いや、目地が強調されているというより、むしろ面と開口が目立つね。
B: 椅子はどのような素材を使用しているの？
A: 椅子は肘かけや背面は硬質な木製だけれど、その他は**肌触りの良い布張り**だよ。
B: 壁も椅子も、木はダークカラーで染色されて、まとまっているね。

....

Q: 木製の壁についてどう思いますか？ホール全体のインテリアにマッチしていると思いますか？

　(e.g.) Although the wooden walls contribute to the sense of unity in terms of color, the space feels heavy at the bottom.
　（木の壁は色の統一感という点では良いのですが、ここでは下部が重く感じられます。）

Unit 3
Material

Dialogue 7　シート素材の検討

A: この表皮は一見グレーだけど、よく見ると差し色に、**光沢のある**糸を使っているね。
B: **ザックリとした**素材感も悪くない。
A: 営業部門へは起毛調で上質感のあるものも提案しておこう。

....

Q: この椅子には他にどのような素材のオプションが考えられますか？
　　(e.g.) Other material options could include organic materials, such as cotton, hemp or silk.
　　　　（他の素材の候補として、綿や麻、シルクなどの有機素材があります。）

Unit 4
Operation

Dialogue 1　<u>回転する</u>ハンドル

A: **ところで、**このドライヤー、**どうやって**持つの？
B: この状態でつかん**でもいい**ですし、持ち手を回転させることもできます。
A: **水平**方向に回転するの？それとも**垂直**？
B: 写真のような状態で垂直方向です。
A: 持ったときの**バランス**が悪くない？

....

Q: Aは、このデザインの何を批判していますか？
Rotating the handle of the hair dryer vertically throws off the balance.
（ドライヤーのハンドルを垂直方向に回転するとバランスが悪くなる点です。）

Unit 4
Operation

Dialogue 2 ボタン**位置**の検討

A: このドリルはどうやって使うのかわからないよ。握りながらボタンを**押す**んだよね？回転の速さの**調節**は**どうするの**？
B: スライドボタンをつけようと思っています。
A: 滑って危なくない？スタートボタンをお尻につけたらどう？上のボタンでスピードを選択して、**押すこと**でスタートさせるようなボタンにしたらどうかな？
B: ありがとうございます。検討してみます。

....

Q: BはAのアドバイスを聞いた後、何を検討するのでしょうか？
B will consider placing the start button on the bottom and the speed select button on top.
（Bは、スタートボタンをお尻につけ、スピード選択ボタンを上につけることを検討します。）

Unit 4
Operation

Dialogue 3　フィードバック

A: この持ち手の**位置**、**造形**的にはきれいだけど、お湯を**注ぐ**ときに力が必要なんじゃないかな？

B: 確かにそうですね。もう少し下の方を支えられるといいかもしれません。

A: 注ぎ口の尻漏りは検証した？

B: いいえ、まだです。これからやります。

....

Q: Aが述べている問題点は何ですか？
A mentions the amount of strength required when pouring the hot water.
（Aは、お湯を注ぐときに力が必要になると述べています。）

Unit 4
Operation

Dialogue 4 外部廊下の役割

A: 外部廊下に活気があるね。
B: (外部廊下は) 教室**から**教室**へと移動する**ときに使うからね。
A: 中庭を回遊するつくりだね。**視線**がゆきかい、アクティビティが誘発されるしかけだな。
B: **滞留する**スペースもあるよ。そこで先生に質問したりできるしね。

....

Q: Aによると、外部廊下は何を目的にデザインされているのですか？
It is designed to offer several lines of sight and encourages activity.
(視線がゆきかい、アクティビティが誘発されるようにデザインされています。)

25

Unit 4
Operation

Dialogue 5 開放感を出す

A: ここのガラス扉からは外部に**出られるの**？
B: 出られるよ。ただ扉の両脇の窓は**開か**ないけどね。
A: その窓も開け放つことができれば、開放感が出そうだね。
B: 自由に**出入りができれば**、内部と外部の一体感が出るね。

....

Q: Bによると、人々が自由に出入りできたらどうなりますか？
There would be a real sense of unity between the interior and exterior.
（内部と外部の一体感がでます。）

Unit 4
Operation

Dialogue 6　車内からの視界

A: こんなにピラーが太いと斜め後方が見にくいのでは？
B: 他社と差別化するためにはこれぐらいに設定する必要があると思うよ。
A: ベンチマークとして比較するため、競合車の数値を調べてみよう。
B: 細くするためには、設計者と交渉が必要だね。

....

Q: Bはデザインについて、どのように擁護していますか？
B defends the design by saying that it is necessary in order to differentiate it from the competition.
（Bは、競合相手との差別化のために必要であるとデザインを擁護しています。）

Unit 5
Composition

Dialogue 1　全体の**構成**

A: 黒の使い方がいいね。白い部分と上手く**対比し**ているよ。ロゴは入れないの？
B: きれいに**まとまっている**だけあって、ロゴを入れるとバランスに影響すると思います。
A: モノトーンだから、赤で**パンチを効かせて**みるのはどうかな？
B: う〜ん。

....

Q: Bは、なぜロゴを入れたくないのでしょう？
　 B doesn't want to add the logo because it might affect the balance between black and white.
　 （Bは、白と黒のバランスに影響するから、ロゴを追加したくありません。）

Unit 5
Composition

Dialogue 2 ロゴの配置

A: このロゴ、スイッチと**センター合わせ**にした方がいいんじゃない？
B: **固めて配置するより**スイッチ**から離した方が**いいと思いますけど。
A: まあ、そうね。オンオフの表示も入れると、要素が多すぎて**ビジーになる**かもね。

・・・

Q: Aは何を提案しましたか？あなたはそれを良いアイデアだと思いますか？
   (e.g.) A suggests aligning the logo with the switch in the center. Although I understand A's point, I think that the logo would become less visible.
   （Aは、ロゴをスイッチと一緒に中央に揃えたいと提案しています。私もAと同じですが、ロゴが目立たなくなると思います。）

Unit 5
Composition

Dialogue 3　建物の配置

A: この建物の配置についてどう思う？
B: 教室は小さい建物の低層部分にまとめてあり、**中庭**は南北の棟に**囲まれている**ね。
A: 2棟を浮遊感のあるガラスのブリッジ**で連結している**し、さらに、中庭の周りに外部廊下が立体的に展開して、回遊性を高めているね。
B: そうだね。ところで、研究室はどこに入っているのかな？
A: 高層棟上部にコンパクトにまとめて、全体構成に**アクセントをつけ**ているよ。機能に応じて棟を構成しているから、わかりやすい計画だと思うよ。

．．

Q: 2つの建物はどのように連結されていますか？
The two buildings are joined together by a glass-covered "floating" bridge and external corridors that expand in three dimensions.
（2棟は、"浮遊感"のあるガラスのブリッジと立体的な外部廊下でつながっています。）

Unit 5
Composition

Dialogue 4　モデルの改良点

A: この案は、全体的に骨格がしっかりしているね。
B: そうだね、とても良い佇まいをしているね。
A: どうすればもっと良くなるかな？
B: 少し要素が多いので、もう少し整理しよう。

....

Q: この案の問題点は何ですか？
　　The problem is that there are a few too many distracting details.
　　（問題点は、少し要素が多くてうるさいところです。）

Unit 5
Composition

Dialogue 5　<u>左右対称の構成</u>

A: 左右対称の構成がすっきりしていていいね。
B: そうかな？ちょっと退屈な感じもするから、**左右非対称**の方がいいんじゃないかな？
A: そんなことないよ。この構成とシックな色を黒で引き締めているところが、日本らしい印象にしているんだよ。
B: なるほどね。

....

Q: Aはこの構成を変えたいと思っていますか？それはなぜですか？
A does not want to change the composition because it is clear and symmetrical.
（Aは、左右対称ですっきりしているから、構成を変更したくありません。）

Unit 5
Composition

Dialogue 6　直感的な操作

A: 操作部の色を赤に統一しているから直感的に操作できるし、梨地のアルミに赤が**効いている**ところがいいね。
B: でも、素材のせいでちょっと冷たい印象も受けるよ。**幾何学的な**形だし。
A: そうかな？すっきりしていて美しいし、中心から伸びた赤いレバーがわずかに湾曲した表面にあって、私は優美な感じがすると思うな。

....

Q: Aは、この作品のどの点を評価していますか？
A thinks having all the operating parts in red make it neat and intuitive. A also thinks that the lever positioned radially onto the slightly curved surface looks elegant.
（Aは、操作部のパーツをすべて赤にしたことが、すっきりさせていて直観的だと思っています。さらにAは、表面が少し湾曲しているうえに、中心から伸びた赤いレバーがあり、優しく感じると思っています。）

Unit 6
Sense

Dialogue 1　女性がターゲット

A: この形、なんだか**和む**ねぇ。
B: はい。女性は電動ドリルに対して**怖い印象を持つ**ことがあるので、**ふわふわの かわいい**小動物のような形にして、**より親しみを感じて**ほしいと思ったんです。
A: それで、モグラにしたの？
B: はい。ドリルで穴を掘る作業がモグラの穴を掘るイメージと合うと思ったので。

....

Q: なぜ B はドリルのモチーフをモグラにしたのですか？
B introduced a mole as a motif for the drill because they hoped it would be thought of as friendlier for women. It was also appropriate because drills make holes, as do moles.
（B は女性に親しみをもってもらいたかったのでモチーフとしました。ドリルはモグラのように穴をあけるので、それもぴったりだと思ったからです。）

Unit 6
Sense

Dialogue 2　その形にした理由

A: いつも部屋に置いておくものなので、小動物のようなかわいい形にして**親しみのある**感じにしながらも、シンプルだけど<u>洗練された**印象を与える**</u>造形にしました。

B: それで鶏**みたいな感じ**にしたの？

A: はい。お茶を入れるために早起きすることを**イメージして**デザインしました。

．．

Q: なぜ A はケトルのモチーフを鶏にしたのですか？
A introduced a rooster as a motif for the kettle because it related to the image of getting up early to prepare the morning tea.
（A は早起きしてお茶を入れるイメージが鶏につながるので、ケトルのモチーフに鶏を採用しました。）

Unit 6
Sense

Dialogue 3　カッコいいスタイリング

A: **うわっ！**これ超カッコイイね！
B: ホントはこんなに**先進的な感じ**じゃなく、もう少しユルイ感じにしたいのだけど。
A: **このまま**の方が、すごく新鮮でいいよ。こんなのどこでも見たことがないもの。

....

Q: Bはこの車についてどう思っていますか？
B feels his design might have too much of an edgy feel. B actually wanted the design to be something a little more loose and gentle.
（Bは、自分のデザインがとんがりすぎていると思っていて、本当はもう少しユルイ感じにしたかったと思っています。）

Unit 6
Sense

Dialogue 4　場の多様性

A: 緑化された屋上は、とてもゆったりとした**開放感**のある場所だね。
B: そうだね。屋上のベンチは、ほっとすることのできる場所だよ。
A: 今はとても**静かで落ち着いた**場所だけれど、イベントのときはずいぶん賑やかになるよね。
B: 祖母が訪れた時、とても活気に満ちた場所ね、と言っていたよ。
A: 一般に開放されているから、さまざまな人が来ることができて、**活気のある**交流の場になっているね。

....

Q: Aが屋上を好きな二つの理由は何ですか？
(e.g.) A likes the dual function of the rooftop. It is usually calm, but it can also be lively on some occasions.
（Aは、普段はゆったりとして落ち着いているけれど、イベントのときには人が集まって生き生きとした交流の場になるという屋上の二面性が好きです。）

37

Unit 7
Scale

Dialogue 1 モック図の縮尺と**寸法**

A: このコーヒーメーカーの**モック図**、**1/2 スケール**で描いても**いいか な**？
B: 問題ないんじゃない？でも、寸法を間違えないように気を付けてね。
A: **そういえば**、B さん、前に片手に収まるコーヒーメーカーの原寸模型を発注してましたね。
B: ああ、そうだよ。やったよ。1/2 スケールの**図面**の大きさを、**原寸 と間違えて**模型を発注しちゃったんだよ。

....

Q: この会話の中で、A が思い出したのはどのようなことでしたか？
A is reminded of the time when B mistook the scale and ordered a mock-up of a coffee maker that could fit in one hand.
（A は、B が以前スケールを間違えて片手に収まるコーヒーメーカーの原寸模型を発注したことを思い出しました。）

Unit 7
Scale

Dialogue 2　大きさ感を出す

A: この時計のアイデアは好きだけど、大きさはどのぐらい？
B: 腕時計ぐらいです。
A: それなら、大きさ感を出すために、それを使っている人の身体も一緒に描くと**良さそうだね**。
B: はい。描いてみます。ところで、1/2スケールで描いていいですか？
A: え？　CADじゃなくて、手描きなの？

....

Q: スケールを把握するために、Aはどのようなことを勧めていますか？
A recommends making a drawing of someone using the watch, so that people can get an idea of what size B had in mind.
（Aは、Bがどのぐらいの大きさをイメージしているのかがわかるよう、人が時計を身につけている絵を描くことを勧めています。）

Unit 7
Scale

Dialogue 3　親和性のあるスケール感

A: キャンパスの規模は大きくても、建物のボリュームは大きくならな**いように計画されているね。**
B: 低層部はさまざまな要素で分割されて、周辺住宅地<u>となじむ</u>スケール感だね。
A: そうだね。見る距離によって建物の表情が変わるように計画されているしね。
B: え？どういう意味？
A: 遠くからは高層棟がランドマークになっていて、近くでは低層部がまわりに**溶け込んでいる**と思わない？

．．．

Q: 周辺環境と調和するためにキャンパスはどのようにデザインされていますか？

To harmonize with the surroundings, the campus has been designed by dividing the lower part of the building into various sections.
（キャンパスは、周辺環境となじむよう、建物の低層部をさまざまな要素に分割してデザインされています。）

Unit 7
Scale

Dialogue 4　安全なディテール

A: 利用者の安全のために、**細部に至るまで**注意深く計画しましょう。
B: 具体的にはどのようなこと？
A: 例えば、コンクリートの柱の角を面取りする。**実際の大きさ**は 1 cm ほどだけれど。
B: 原寸模型で検討しないといけない内容だね。**図面**では何分の一の縮尺で表現しますか。

....

Q: なぜデザイナーは、詳細まで注意深く計画しなければならないのでしょうか？
The designers have to plan carefully down to the smallest detail in order to make sure the design is safe for the user.
（デザイナーは、利用者の安全を確実にするために、細部の至るところまで注意深く計画しなければなりません。）

Unit 7
Scale

Dialogue 5　スケッチの**スケール感**

A: このスケッチだと、<u>実</u>車のスケール感がわからないね。
B: 一応軽自動車のつもりだけど。
A: **そうは見えないよ**。もっとボディーとタイヤのバランスを考えて描かないと。

....

Q: スケッチを見た人がスケールを把握できるようにするために、B にどのように描くことを A は提案していますか？
In order to comprehend the scale, A suggests B should draw it considering the balance between the body and the wheels.
（スケール感を把握することができるよう、A は B にボディーとタイヤのバランスを考えて描くように提案しています。）

Unit 8
Situation

Dialogue 1　新たなターゲット

A: この工具は、**20代〜30代の**女性で、手作り雑貨好きだけど、**DIY**に関しては**初心者**という人に使ってもらうこと**を想定しています**。
B: DIYってたいていお父さんや旦那さんがやることなんじゃないの？
A: 一人暮らしを始めたばかりの女性**が**ターゲット**です**。かっこいい工具にしたら家具を組み立てるときに、楽しく組み立てられるんじゃないかな、と思っています。

．．．

Q: この製品をターゲットにとってより魅力的なものとするために、他にどのようなアイデアがありますか？
　　(e.g.) The product could be more appealing if it were named after a cute animal.
　　　　（製品にかわいい動物の名前がついていれば、より魅力的になるでしょう。）

Unit 8
Situation

Dialogue 2 状況に応じたデザイン

A: エアコンのダイヤル**の件だけど**、小さ過ぎて、運転中は使いづらいね。
B: **そうだね**、ドライバーには<u>高齢者</u>も多いからそこは**改善が必要だね**。暗いときに文字を光らせるのはどうかな？
A: それはよさそうだね。デジタル表示を使うのはどうかな？高齢者には使いづらいかもしれないけど。

....

Q: 高齢ドライバーのために配慮すべきデザインは、若手ドライバーのためのデザインとどのように違いますか？
Older drivers need instrumentation that is clear and easy to read.
（高齢ドライバーは、大きく見やすい機器を必要とします。）

Unit 8
Situation

Dialogue 3　敷地条件と計画

A: この大学の特徴は、都市部に**位置している**ことです。小学校や公園**に隣接して**、教育文化ゾーンを形成しています。
B: キャンパスは、周辺環境と**調和している**かな？
A: はい。低層部は**周辺のスカイライン**と連続しています。ただ、高層棟は周辺地域のランドマークになっているけど、突出している印象もあります。
B: でも、緑豊かなキャンパスにして**アクセスしやすく**し、周辺地域と馴染んだ空間を目指しているのはわかるね。

....

Q: 都市部に近い大学はどんなところが便利ですか？
Events held at the university are easily accessible to the public.
（イベント開催時にお客様のアクセスが良いところです。）

45

Unit 8
Situation

Dialogue 4　場所と利用者

A: キャンパス南側の、道路に**面する**部分の1階に工房があるね。
B: この工房は、**どのように**使われているの？
A: 学生**専用**の場所というわけではなく、地域住民**を対象とした**場所だよ。
B: 地域住民って、どんな世代の人の利用が多いのかな？
A: 退職後のアクティブシニアが多そうなイメージがあるなぁ。

....

Q: あなたは道路に面する部屋をどのような用途に利用するのが良いと思いますか？
　(e.g.) I think a room facing the road is good for classes that are open to the public, because it is easily accessible.
　（私は、道路に面した部屋は公開講座に使うのがいいと思います。なぜなら、アクセスしやすいからです。）

Unit 9
Light and Shadow

Dialogue 1　照明効果の検討

A: 素材を**透過**した光が美しい**影**を創ります。
B: 調光はできるの？
A: はい。**光量**とシェードの角度の両方で調光することによって、好みの影を演出できます。
B: 直接床を**照らす**のもいいけど、天井や壁に光を向けて、間接照明にしてもいいかもね。

．．

Q: 自然光は人工の光とどのように異なりますか？
Natural light differs from artificial light in that it is more difficult to control. The use of artificial light allows for greater control of the quantity of light, the angle of the shadow and its position.
（自然光は、人工の光にくらべて調整するのが難しいですが、人工の光は、光の量や影の角度、そして位置を調整することができます。）

47

Unit 9
Light and Shadow

Dialogue 2 建物における光と<u>影</u>

A: <ruby>庇<rt>ひさし</rt></ruby>が壁に繊細な影を**落としている**のがいいね。
B: たくさんのスリットで分割しているからだね。
A: そうだね。窓面への**日差し**を遮ったり、外壁にリズミカルな影をもたらしたりするね。
B: 室内に**降り注ぐ**光の量を調節し、明るく快適な空間を作っているね。

....

Q: この建物の場合、<ruby>庇<rt>ひさし</rt></ruby>がどのような効果をもたらしていますか？
The canopy provides shade from the sun and also projects a pleasant rhythmical shadow on the outer wall.
（この<ruby>庇<rt>ひさし</rt></ruby>のおかげで、日避けの効果と、リズミカルで心地よい影が外壁に演出されています。）

Unit 9
Light and Shadow

Dialogue 3　光の**反射**と車の表面

A: ショルダーの部分がうまく光るように角度を調整したんだ。
B: 映り込みもキレイで、**カタチの意図**がよく伝わるね。

....

Q: カーデザイナーは、ボディーの**光**の反射に関してどのような要素を考える必要がありますか？
　(e.g.) Car designers need to consider how the sunlight's reflection affects the appearance of a car shape.
　　（カーデザイナーは、光の反射によって形が違って見えることを考慮しなければなりません。）

Unit 9
Light and Shadow

Dialogue 4　明るさと判読性

A: このサイン、設置場所が暗すぎて、文字が読めないね。
B: 読めるように明るい場所に置かないとだめだよ。高齢者には白内障の人が多いからさらに読みにくいよね。もっと配慮するべきでは？
A: じゃあ、スポットライトを**当て**てはどうかな？それともパネルを発光させる？
B: 文字を**蛍光**素材で描くというのはどう？
A: まずは、サンプルを作って確認してみよう。

....

Q: 文字を読みやすくするために、他にどのような方法がありますか？
　　(e.g.) The lettering could be made of glow-in-the-dark material.
　　　　（蓄光素材で文字を描きます。）

Unit 9
Light and Shadow

Dialogue 5　照明の効果

A: 照明って、**直接**と**間接**とでは全く違う効果が出て面白いよね。
B: そうだね、同じ直接照明でも、集中させるのと**拡散**させるのでは機能が違ってくるしね。
A: だから、**望まれる効果**を得るためには工夫して使うことが必要だよね。
B: なるほど。浴室の明かりを間接照明にしてリラックスするとか、ヒゲを剃るときなどは直接照明で明るくするとか。
A: 他にも、お店がお客さまを惹きつけるために、華やかに**照らし出された**看板を使うこともあるね。
B: もっといろいろな効果を調べてみよう。

....

Q: この会話によると、間接照明は、その機能を発揮するためにどのように使われることがありますか？
Indirect lighting can be used in the bath to create a relaxing effect.
（間接照明は、リラックス効果を演出するために、浴室で使われることがあります。）

Unit 10
Function

Dialogue 1 荷室の素材

A: 荷室を**拡大し**たので**使いやすくなった**けど、コストが高くても**汚れにくい**素材を用いるべきだったね。
B: そうだね、ユーザーのクレームを防止するためにも、今後の課題としよう。

....

Q: このスペースには、どのような素材が**ふさわしい**と思いますか？
   (e.g.) It should be made of material that is water resistant and easy to clean.
   （防水加工が施されていて掃除しやすい素材でできているといいですね。）

Unit 10
Function

Dialogue 2　屋上庭園の効能

A: 大規模な屋上緑化だよね。うねっているから自然環境を**強調し**ているよ。
B: どうしてこうしたんだろう？環境上の理由かな？
A: そうだね。屋上緑化は、ヒートアイランドなどの建物が与える環境への**負荷を低減する**効果があるからね。
B: 室内**にも**効果はある？
A: 室内には、外部からの熱負荷を低減する断熱効果があるよ。
B: 建物内部**にも**、周辺の都市地域**にも**、効果があるんだね。

....

Q:　この屋上庭園はどのように維持されるべきでしょうか？
　　(e.g.) It needs to be regularly weeded and an image of a pleasant verdant garden needs to be maintained.
　　（定期的に雑草を取り除いて、快適な状態の緑を絶やさないようにするべきでしょう。）

Unit 10
Function

Dialogue 3　飲み物の容器

A: この袋は、飲み終わった後にコンパクトに**畳んで**簡単に**収納する**ことができます。
B: 何か問題はありませんか？たとえば**衛生**面はどうですか？
A: 問題ありません。口の部分を広げると、飲み物を入れやすい**だけでなく**、洗浄しやすくなります。また、シリコンを使用すれば、熱湯で消毒することも可能です。
B: でも、汚れが落ちにくかったり**繰り返しの使用**で口の部分が伸びてしまったりしないのですか？
A: **確かに** …… 素材については、再検討してみます。

....

Q: A はなぜ素材の再検討をしようとしているのですか？
A wants to test the material again because there is a possibility that some liquids could stain it, or repeated use could cause the opening to stretch.
（A は、入れる液体によってはシミを作ったり、繰り返し使うことで開口部が広がってしまったりする可能性があるため、素材を再検討したいと思っています。）

Unit 10
Function

Dialogue 4　映画鑑賞の新提案

A: これはパーソナルなムービーシアターということだね。
B: そうなんです。一般的な映画館のような機能があり、自由に我がままに楽しめます。
A: 自宅でDVDを観るのとは違って、**快適**な椅子と質の高い音響システムのおかげでストーリーに**没頭**できるね。
B: さらに大きなモデルもあって、2人あるいはそれ以上で感動をシェアする体験**も**できます。
A: 個別の鑑賞ブースの外観が鑑賞中の映画を表示することで広告塔に**もなっている**ね。
B: そうなんです。体験してみたくなってきましたか？

....

Q: この新しい映画館は、普通のものと何が違いますか？
This new kind of movie theater allows you to enjoy the movie on your own and become more easily immersed in the story. Larger versions could allow two or more people to also share in the experience.
(この新しい映画館は、自分一人で映画を楽しんだり、ストーリーに没頭しやすくしたりできます。大きいタイプは、2人以上の人と体験を共有することができます。)

Unit 11
Application

Competition 1　応募要項

20th UAC Campus Goods Award
テーマ：知と美を伝えるギフトグッズ
UACをアピールするための知的で美しいグッズ

賞：グランプリ 100万円、部門賞 10万円
部門：ノベルティ部門、販売部門
募集対象：文房具、その他のギフト商品
応募資格：個人、グループ、企業、団体。年齢、性別、職業、国籍は問わない。
　　　　　　未発表のものであることを条件とする。
審査員：静岡文汰、浜松ゲーテ、空田海子
審査方法：**一次審査**／プレゼンテーションシートによる書類審査
　　　　　　最終審査／模型とパネルによるプレゼンテーション
審査基準：大学グッズとしてふさわしいもの、持ち運べるもの、美しいもの、**商品化が可能なもの**

スケジュール：
エントリー／2016年10月1日〜2016年11月1日（仮登録）
一次審査／2016年11月末　通過者のみに連絡
最終審査用作品提出／2016年12月25日必着。最終審査はパネルと模型により審査を行う。
結果発表／本人に直接通知。2017年2月1日Web上にて公開。

Unit 11
Application

Competition 1　応募用紙

一次審査　プレゼンテーションシート（表）

二重線より上に応募者を特定できる情報を記載しないこと。

1. 作品タイトル

   ティー・ブレイク（しおり）

2. 応募部門

   ノベルティ部門

3. コンセプト（200ワード以内）

   お茶の葉をモチーフにした木製ブックマーク。しおりを挟む動作によってお茶の芳香を放つ。読書の合間のほんのちょっとした休憩中、ティーブレイクのようなリラックスした感覚にさせる。

氏名：浜　みか
グループ名（個人の場合は記載不要）：ORANGE
住所：松浜市丘区 11 − 11
Eメールアドレス：mmt@uac.ac.jp
職業：大学生

Unit 11
Application

一次審査　プレゼンテーションシート（裏）

4. 図：3D-CG、模型写真、イラスト等（大きさの分かる寸法を記入のこと）

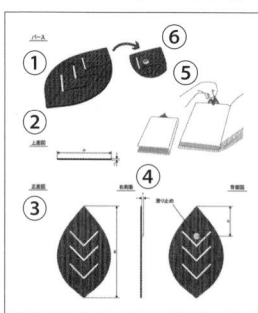

①パース
②上面図
③正面図
④側面図
⑤使用状況
⑥裏面すべり止め

Q. 応募する前に以下の項目について書き出してみましょう。

1. このコンペティションはどんな作品の応募を求めていますか？
   Intelligent and beautiful gift items that promote UAC (to the surrounding community)
   （UACをアピールするための知的で美しいグッズ）
2. 最終審査用提出物の締め切りはいつですか？
   December 25, 2016.（2016年12月25日）
3. 一次審査はどのように行われますか？
   Based on presentation sheet
   （プレゼンテーションシートによる書類審査）
4. 最終審査はどのように行われますか？
   Based on design model and panel
   （模型とパネルによる審査）
5. 審査結果はどのように通知されますか？
   Contacted directly and posted on website
   （本人への直接通知とWeb上で公開される）

Unit 11
Application

Competition 2　応募要項

40th UAC City Award
テーマ：まちなかを潤すモニュメント
街を再活性化させるためのしかけの提案

主催：UAC市まちなか組合／後援：株式会社芸術
賞：最優秀賞（1点）200万円及び記念品、優秀賞（2点）各30万円
審査員：山田太郎、文芸花子、野口一郎

一次審査
登録方法：事前登録が必要。インターネットにより登録、運営局に登録票を
　　　　　送付。
提出図面：平面図、断面図、配置図（縮尺自由）、透視図もしくは模型写真、
　　　　　その他設計意図を表現する説明文や図。（説明文は100字以内）
用紙：A2判（全ての図面、イラスト、文を厚手ケント紙1枚に配置すること。）
　　　パネル化不可。
提出方法：裏面に登録票を貼付の上、郵送のこと。持込み不可。

スケジュール
事前登録：2016年4月1日〜2016年4月15日
応募締切：2016年6月1日。当日消印有効。
一次審査結果発表：2016年7月上旬。通過者に通知。

最終審査
公開最終審査：一次審査通過作品について、**最終審査**を公開面接方式で行う。
最終審査結果発表：審査の結果は、月刊「文化芸術」2016年10号に発表。

その他
・応募作品は未発表の作品に限る。
・規定に関する質疑は受け付けない。
・応募に関する費用は全て応募者の負担とする。
・応募作品は返却しない。
・受賞した応募作品の著作権は応募者に帰属するが、雑誌やTVへの作品の
　発表に関する権利は主催者側が保有する。

Unit 11
Application

Competition 2　提出書類

一次審査　提出図面記載事項（A2 判用紙 1 枚）

1. 作品タイトル

    成長する庭

2. 設計趣旨（コンセプト）

    人と共に時間を経て育つ庭を提案する。敷地は商店街入り口にある広場状の空地。無数の円盤状の石の床が池の中に浮く。時間と共に庭は成長し、花が豊かに咲く。庭の成長と共に、街がにぎわう計画である。

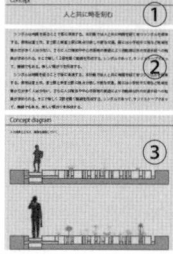

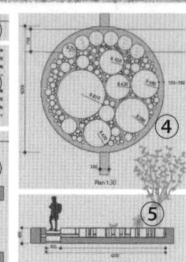

3. コンセプトダイアグラム

4. 配置図兼平面図（縮尺 1:30）

5. 断面図（縮尺 1:30）

Unit 11
Application

一次審査　登録票（裏面に貼布）

氏名（グループの場合代表者名）　　浜 みか
勤務先または学校名（学年）　　　　文化芸術大学（4年）
年齢　　　　　　　　　　　　　　　22 歳
住所　　　　　　　　　　　　　　　松浜市丘区 11 − 11
E-mail アドレス　　　　　　　　　　mmt@uac.ac.jp
作者経歴（100 ワード以内）
浜みか。文化芸術大学デザイン学部 4 年生。空間デザインを**専攻して**おり、環境に優しいビルに**焦点を当て**た建築に特に**興味を持っている**。2014 年 SSS 空間大賞最優秀賞受賞。環境と調和したよりよい生活のための**デザインを目指し**ている。

Activities

Unit 1　Color

Activity 1　ベストドレッサー / Best Dresser

【解答例】

I think the color coordination of person A is the best. The grey jacket over a white shirt balances well with her navy-blue pants, and it is accentuated by the thin waist belt. It harmonizes well with her light brown hair and the chic ensemble makes her look mature.

彼女 A のコーディネートが一番素敵だと思います。白いシャツの上に着たグレーのジャケットと紺色のパンツのバランスが取れているし、腰の細いベルトがコーディネートを引き締めているからです。また、彼女の明るい茶色の髪色とも調和が取れていてシックな全体の感じが彼女を大人っぽく見せています。

Unit 1 Color

Activity 2　ロゴマーククイズ / Logo Mark Quiz

【解答例】

Logo 1: This logo is a blue square with curved lines on all four sides. It looks like a flag waving in the wind. Four capital letters are written below the square.

ロゴ1: このマークは4辺を曲線で構成された青い四角形です。まるで旗が風にそよいでいるような形です。下に4つの大文字があります。

Logo 2: This logo consists of three circles extending upward to the right. However, the bottom two are not full circles, they are more like crescent moons; only the top one is a full circle. The bottom crescent moon is green. The crescent moon above it is grey and a little less full than the green one below. The one on top is a brilliant red and is the only full circle.

ロゴ2: このロゴは、右上に上がっていく3つの円で構成されています。しかし、下の2つは正円ではなく三日月のようであり、つまり一番上だけが正円です。一番下の三日月は緑色です。その上の三日月はグレーで、下の緑色のものより薄く（細く）なっています。一番上のものだけが鮮やかな赤で、正円になっています。

Logo 3: There is a coffee bean in the middle at the bottom. It forms the bottom of the vertically-oval shape of the logo. There is text going up and around making the rest of the oval. On the left side starting from the bottom, the brand name is written in capital letters. "Since 1999" is written on the right side. For this text, only the "s" is capitalized.

ロゴ3: 下部中央にコーヒー豆があります。それは、縦に長い楕円の下部にあり、回り込んだ文字が残りの楕円の部分を構成しています。下から始まる左側のブランドネームは、大文字で書かれています。"Since 1999" と創業年が右側に書かれています。この文字は最初の文字が大文字になっています。

Activities

Unit 1　Color

Activity 3　ツートーンボディーカラー / Two-Tone Body Color

【解答例】

[A: color designer　　B: production engineer]

A: I'd like to talk about the two-tone color combination of the body and roof.
B: Factory production for the roof is not set for more than two colors.
A: What? Young people won't buy it if they can't choose the color. It was originally designed as a two-tone car. Besides, our competitors offer a greater selection of colors.
B: They do what they do, we do what we do.
A: Let's see. What should we do? I guess we have to change the plan a little.
B: Where? Show me. What? Nice! I'll make it work with the equipment we have and see that it gets painted.
A: Awesome. It's great working with you.

A: ボディーとルーフのツートーンの組み合わせについて相談したいのですが。
B: 工場で生産の都合上、ルーフ色の設定は２色までだね。
A: ええっ？色が選べないと若い人が買ってくれないですよ。そもそもツートーンを前提にしたデザインだし、それに競合他社はもっと多くの色から選べますよ。
B: ヨソはヨソ、ウチはウチだよ。
A: まいったなぁ。それでは計画を変更しなければ。
B: どれどれ？ちょっと見せてごらん。おっ！これはいいじゃないか！よーし、何とか設備のやりくりをして、塗れるようにしてやろう。
A: やったー！さすが話がわかる！

Unit 2　Form

Activity 4　ショールームでのやり取り / Give and Take at a Showroom

【解答例】

[A: salesperson　　B: customer]

A: This car was just released last month. The wedge shape is very sporty. If you look at it from the front, you can see how the tires fold out in the four corners, and it looks solid.
B: It definitely looks cool, but I wonder if it is suitable for someone my age. The lights are too high. And doesn't the front look a little scary?
A: No, this shape is the trend right now. And because it uses LED headlights, it attracts a lot of attention at night .
B: If the lights were more round, it would be cuter. This pink color is too showy.
A: I don't think it is too showy at all. I think it really fits you. Also, the body is available in ten different colors.
B: You really think so? I think you're just trying to flatter me. But it's working.

A: お客様、こちらが先月発売されたばかりの車です。ウエッジシェイプでスポーティーなデザインとしています。正面から見ると、タイヤが四隅に踏ん張って安定感があるのがよくわかると思います。
B: 確かにカッコイイけど私の年齢ではどうかしらね。それに目が吊り上がって、顔が怖く見えない？
A: いえ、こういうデザインが最新のトレンドです。ヘッドライトにLEDを使っているので、夜も目立ちますよ。
B: 私はもっと丸いカワイイ目が好きなんだけど。このピンクも派手過ぎて……。
A: 全然派手じゃないですよ。お客様にピッタリだと思います。それにボディーカラーは10色の中からお選びいただけます。
B: 本当にそう思う？あなたお世辞言ってるんじゃない。やるわね。

Activities

Unit 3 Material

Activity 5 製品の素材 / Product Materials

【解答例】
A: First, what are the positives when paper plates are used instead of regular ones.
B: You don't need to wash paper plates, because they are cheap and easily disposable. That makes them suitable for parties or outdoor events. They are also very light and easy to carry.
A: Do they have any negative points?
B: Well, they aren't very water resistant, and they look a little cheap.
A: How about plastic plates?
B: Plastic plates are definitely more water resistant, relatively inexpensive and more durable than paper plates, but they also look a little cheap. Also, both are affected by heat, so it is not easy to hold hot items on them.
A: When you think about it, regular ceramic plates have a good balance of price, look, durability, and thermal conductivity. What about their disadvantages?
B: They are heavy and crack or chip easily, so they must be handled with care.

A: では、まず、お皿に紙を使ったらどういうメリットがあると思いますか？
B: 紙製の皿は、安価で使い捨てることができるので洗わずに済むことを考えると、パーティーやアウトドアでの使用に向いていると思います。軽いから持ち運びも楽ですし。
A: 短所についてはどうですか？
B: やはり耐水性が低いことと、何と言っても見た目が安っぽいですね。
A: プラスチック製のものはどうですか？
B: 耐水性もあり、比較的安価で壊れにくいですね。でも、やはり少し安っぽいかな。さらに、どちらも熱に関しては、熱いものを入れると持ちにくいという欠点もあります。
A: そういった意味で、陶器の器は価格、見た目、耐久性、熱伝導性などのバランスがいいと言えますね。欠点を上げるとすれば何ですか？
B: 重いことと割れやすく欠けやすいところかな。だから、慎重に扱わないといけないですしね。

皿 plates/dishes			
		長所 positives	短所 negatives
紙 paper		安い cheap 軽い light 使い捨てできる disposable	耐水性が低い not water resistant 安っぽい looks cheap 熱伝導性 thermal conductivity (not easy to carry hot items)
プラスチック plastic		耐水性 water resistant 安価 inexpensive 耐久性が高い durable 材料着色 colored materials	安っぽい looks cheap 熱伝導性 thermal conductivity (not easy to carry hot items)
陶磁器 ceramic		耐水性 water resistant 安価 inexpensive 耐久性が高い durable 熱伝導性 thermal conductivity 耐熱性 heat resistant	重い heavy 割れやすい easily broken
ガラス glass		耐水性 water resistant 透明 transparent (content are visible) 美しいカット加工 beautifully cut	壊れやすい fragile 汚れが目立つ dirt shows up 熱伝導性 thermal conductivity (not easy to carry hot items) 耐熱性 heat resistant
金属 metal		耐水性 water resistant 耐久性が高い durable 耐熱性 heat resistant	熱伝導性 thermal conductivity (not easy to carry hot items) 味への影響 affects the taste 歯が当たったときの感触 affects the teeth

Activities

Unit 4 Operation

Activity 6   取り扱い説明 / Directions

【解答例】

Compass ／コンパス

When you use this product, first of all, open the two legs, and holding with your fingers at the fulcrum, place the pointed end on the page and rotate the other leg around, drawing a circle.

この製品を使うときにはまず、二つの足を開き、中央の持ち手部分を指で持ちます。針のついた足を紙に刺し、もう片方の足を回転させて、円を描きます。

Iron ／アイロン

First, remove the detachable water tank and fill it with water to the MAX line on the tank. Return the water-filled tank to its position. Turn the power switch on, then push the sliding button and hold it until the red light turns blue. A beeping noise indicates when it is ready for use. Grasp by the handle and press onto the desired area. As necessary, it is also possible to press the top button to release steam.

まず、着脱式水タンクを取り外し、規定量の線まで水を入れます。タンクをもとの位置にセットします。電源スイッチを押し、設定温度までスライダーを動かしたら、赤色のインジケータが青色になるまで待ちます。音がしたら、使用可能です。ハンドル部分を持ち、対象物に押し当ててください。必要に応じて、上部のボタンを押してスチームを噴射することも可能です。

Unit 4 Operation

Activity 7　昔のテレビ / An Old TV

【解答例】

[A: son　　B: father]

A: Wow! Where did you find this antique? In olden days, people had to turn the knob to change channels and push the switches. All the functions had to be controlled from the body of the TV.

B: It was much easier to use than having to choose from many functions with a remote control, like now. When I was a child, I had to use the newspaper to check what TV program I wanted to watch, then I stretched out my arm to turn to the program, and I sat back and relaxed.

A: Hmm, sounds like a lot of work. Oh no! The screen went black!

B: It'll get better if you hit it. Careful! Not so hard or you'll knock it over!

A: うわぁ、どこでそんな骨董品を見つけてきたの？昔のテレビはチャンネルを回したり、スイッチを押したり、全部本体で操作するんだね。

B: そうだよ、今のようにリモコンで機能を選択するより、余程使いやすいよ。お父さんが子どもの頃は、新聞を拡げて見たい番組を選び、手を伸ばしてつまみをひねったら、寝転がって見たものさ。

A: ふーん、何だか面倒だね。あれっ！画面が消えちゃったよ。

B: なぁに、ちょっと叩けばすぐ直るさ。おいおい、そんな乱暴にやるとひっくり返るじゃないか！

Activities

Unit 5 Composition

Activity 8　ショッピングモールにて / At a Shopping Mall

【解答例】

[A, B: architecture student]

A: This shopping mall is divided into several zones, and was designed so that customers can easily find what they want.
B: The zones have a certain rhythm, each with their own strengths and weaknesses, but overall complementing one another.
A: I feel the composition needs stronger contrast.
B: Well, the entire mall is based on a basic module, so I'm not surprised that you feel that way.
A: Ok. Anyway, time for the food court!

A: このショッピングモールは、ゾーンに分けて建物を配置することで、客が目的の売り場を見つけやすく構成されているね。
B: どのゾーンも強弱のある構成でリズム感があって、お互いを引き立てあっているね。
A: 強いて言えば、構成にもう少しメリハリがあると引き締まると思うのだけど……。
B: そうだね、モール全体が基本モジュールで構成されているから、そう思うのも無理はないと思うよ。
A: さぁ、とにかくそろそろフードコートへ行こうぜ！

Unit 6 Sense

Activity 9　対照的なイメージ / Image Contrast

【解答例】

I think person A is wearing a masculine military-style jacket that makes the wearer appear tough and strong, able to survive in the rugged outdoors. On the other hand, person B is wearing black rimmed glasses and urban chic clothing that projects a slender silhouette, similar to that of a librarian.

Aはハードなミリタリー調のジャケットを着ていて、タフで強く、どんな荒野でもサバイバルできそうです。それとは対照的に、Bは、インテリっぽい黒縁メガネと細身のシルエットの服が都会的かつおしゃれな感じで、図書館が似合いそうです。

Activities

Unit 6 Sense

Activity 10   好きな理由 / Reasons for Liking Something

【解答例】

I prefer the orange color of this car. It looks lively and fun, and using it to go places is likely to make the adventure more exiting. The orange body color and the white fender complement the casual-style of the car. However, I really don't like the grey car. The color doesn't match with the cutesy styling. Overall, it doesn't look overly modern, so I think seniors may find the familiar design comforting.

この車のオレンジが好きです。元気で楽しそうで、遊びに行くときの高揚感を高めてくれそうです。オレンジのボディーと白いフェンダーが、車のカジュアル感とマッチしています。一方、このグレーの車は私の好みではありません。可愛らしいスタイリングと合わないように思います。でも、全体的にとても野暮ったい感じはしますが、年配の方には安心感を与えるかもしれません。

Unit 6 Sense

Activity 11　色のイメージ / Color Image

【解答例】

Lipstick ／口紅

The dark red of this lipstick would look good on an elegant adult woman. This pinkish-beige color looks earthy and natural, and would be suitable for office attire. This pale bright pink color over here would make me look cheerful and cute, so I'd like to wear it when I am on a date.

この口紅の濃い赤はエレガントで大人の女性に似合いそうですね。ちょっとベージュがかったピンクは、落ち着いていて自然な印象だからオフィスでも使えそうです。この淡いピンクは、明るくて可愛らしい印象に見えそうだから、デートのときに使いたいです。

Activities

Unit 6 Sense

Activity 12　建築物の印象 / Architecture Impression

【解答例】

The Guggenheim and MoMA are two classic examples of New York City museums. Designed by Frank Lloyd Wright and constructed in 1959, the unique and beautiful design of the Guggenheim Museum appears futuristic even today. One of the main features of the museum is its spiral structure. More than the architecture, it is the simple carved sculpture that makes it a landmark of the city streets.

In 2004, the Museum of Modern Art renovation by Yoshio Taniguchi was designed as a miniature garden for the surrounding buildings in New York. Visitors can appreciate the sculptures in natural light against the backdrop of the neighboring skyscrapers. It is clear that the garden was designed to emphasize the view from the inside. For visitors, this sculpture garden acts as a peaceful oasis amidst the hubbub of the city.

ニューヨークの代表的な美術館であるグッゲンハイム美術館と MoMA。
フランク・ロイド・ライトによるグッゲンハイムは、1959 年建造にもかかわらず、現代においても未来を感じるユニークで美しい建築です。らせん状の構造が特徴的なこの美術館は、建築というよりは彫刻的な外観がストリートのシンボルとなっています。

2004 年に谷口吉生の設計により改修された MoMA は、ニューヨークのビル群の箱庭のような空間になっています。来訪者は摩天楼をバックに自然光のもとで彫刻を眺めることができます。中庭が内側からの眺めを強調するように設計されたであろうことは明らかです。この彫刻の中庭は都市の喧騒の中にあって、オアシスのような役割を果たします。

Unit 7 Scale

Activity 13　図面のスケール / The Scale of Drawings

【解答】
1) When drawing something that a person can hold in their hand, such as a hair dryer, normally you draw on a scale of < 1/1 >.
2) Things that are small and made with great detail, such as wristwatches, are drawn on a scale of < 2/1 >.
3) A model of a car is made on a scale of < 1/5 > or < 1/10 >.
4) When drawing with CAD, one should enter the figures on a scale of < 1/1 >.
5) In an architectural floor plan for houses, the dimensions are shown on a scale of < 1/100 >.
6) In architectural drawings related to city planning, one may draw on a scale of < 1/1000 >.
7) 5cm on a < 1/2 > drawing is 10cm in actual size.

Activities

Unit 8 Situation

Activity 14 ターゲットと使用シーン / Target and Scene

【解答例】

[A, B: designer]

A: Who is the target user for this product?
B: Girl students who are sensitive to trendy products, or single women who like cute things.
A: Ok, in what setting do you think this product would be used?
B: Umm, club members gathering after school to practice dancing outside. Or to put on a table for when kids are studying together. Female office workers might think it is cool just to have one.
A: You mean there are those who would buy one but not use it?
B: There are more people like that than you think.
A: Really? Ok, well, what are the negative points of this product?
B: The product is fine, but there might be a problem with market share. Niche products like this don't sell in large numbers, and they go out of style fairly quickly.

A: この商品の想定されるターゲットは、誰かな？
B: 流行に敏感な女子学生じゃないかな？それか、可愛い物好きの独身女性。
A: じゃあ、どんな場面で使われると思う？
B: ん〜、放課後に部活仲間がダンスの練習のために屋外で使うとか。ほかには、子どもたちが一緒に勉強しているときに机の上に置くとか？ OL だったら、ただ持っているだけでかっこいいと思うんじゃないかな？
A: つまり、使わないのに買う人がいるってこと？
B: 意外とそういう人が多いんじゃないかな？
A: へええ。じゃあ、この商品に想定される問題点は何かある？
B: 商品そのものというより、マーケットに問題があると思うな。マーケットがニッチだから販売台数は少なさそうだし、すぐに流行遅れになりそうだよ。

Unit 8 Situation

Activity 15　どのネクタイが好き？ / Which Ties Do You Like?

【解答例】

[A: salesperson　B: customer]

A: I think that a tie with this polka dot pattern matches your shirt.
B: Mmm, the pattern is nice but it is a little too plain.
A: Then how about an animal motif pattern, or an ethnic pattern? This one is on sale now.
B: Hmm. No, I'm sorry. This one doesn't do it for me either. Don't you have anything more ... interesting?
A: Well, if interesting is what you want, how about a cartoon-character pattern, like this?
B: That's great, but I don't think it's acceptable to wear at a formal event.

A: お客様のシャツには、この水玉模様のネクタイが似合うと思います。
B: うーん、上品だけど普通過ぎてつまらないなぁ。
A: では動物をモチーフにした柄とか、エスニック調の柄とかはいかがでしょう？こちらはお買得となっております。
B: いや、ごめんなさい。まだしっくり来ないなぁ。もっと面白いやつはないの？
A: もし面白いものがよろしければ、このような漫画のキャラクターの柄はどうですか？
B: おっ、いいねぇ！でも正式な行事にはして行けないなぁ。

77

Activities

Unit 8 Situation

Activity 16 建築家とクライアント / Client & Architect

【解答例】

[A: client   B: architect]

A: The site in the mountains has a great view of the sea! But the train access isn't very good.

B: If you decide on this site, we can build the house facing the sea with an open view. It will be a really relaxing place to live.

A: But my wife told me she wants to live in a place near the station so she can travel easily to the city. She is a huge fan of the theater.

B: Well, this site actually used to be a theater. If you like it, how about designing a house the style of a theater? What do you think?

A: この敷地は山の中腹にあって、海を見おろして見晴らしがとてもいいんだ。駅からのアクセスはあまりよくないけどね。

B: ここなら、海に向かって視線が開けた家ができますね。くつろげる場所になりますよ。

A: だけど、妻は、街に出やすいように駅に近い場所に住みたいと言うんだ。妻は演劇を見るのが好きだからね。

B: 実は、ここにはかつて劇場が建っていたんですよ。もしお好きなら劇場みたいな家はいかがですか？

Unit 9　Light and Shadow

Activity 17　目覚まし時計の表示 / Alarm Clock Display

【解答例】

A: Do you have any ideas for an alarm clock display that will tell the time in the dark?
B: We could make the numbers on the LCD brighter.
A: But if the clock is in a bright room, it will be hard to read. How about using a backlight?
B: Even without an LCD, we can paint clock hands with glow-in-the-dark material such as light storage coating?
A: I see. How about using the lighting in terms of universal design?
B: If the display flashes at the same time the alarm is sounding, it might be useful for the visually or hearing impaired.
A: That's true. And if might be helpful for people who have trouble getting up in the morning.
B: Yes, but I don't want to go too far. For those who want to be woken up slowly or don't like bright lights at night, there should be a function for adjusting the display to dim-light or gradual lighting mode.

A: 暗闇でも時間がわかるような目覚まし時計の表示のアイデアはないかな？
B: 液晶表示にして数字を光らせるとか？
A: 液晶表示は明るい部屋にある時は見づらそうだね。バックライトはどう？
B: 液晶表示にしなくても、針に蓄光塗料を塗れば暗いところでも光るんじゃない？
A: なるほど。光を使って何かユニバーサルデザインへの配慮はできるかな？
B: 音と同時に画面が激しく点滅すれば、視覚や聴覚に障害がある人も気が付きやすいんじゃないかな？
A: そうだね。なかなか起きられない人にも効果がありそうだね。
B: そんな刺激的な起き方はしたくないなぁ。ゆっくり起こしてほしい人とか夜中に明るい光を見たくない人用に、ぼんやり光るモードとかだんだん明るくなるように調整できるような機能も付けたいな。

Activities

Unit 9 Light and Shadow

Activity 18 暮らしと照明 / Lifestyle and Lighting

【解答例】
A: What kind of lighting would you choose for the dining area?
B: I think a simple ceiling light to illuminate the entire room together with pendant lighting for the table would be best.
A: What kind of lighting colors illuminate the best? For example, fluorescent or incandescent lighting color?
B: Fluorescent lights are bright enough for the dining room, but they are a little too cold, so regular incandescent lighting is better. In the kitchen, fluorescent lights make it easier for people to see the color and condition of the food that they are preparing.
A: How about the living room?
B: Adding floor lights to the chandelier enhances the elegant atmosphere of a living room where people can relax. For the chandelier, I want to choose one that is Art Nouveau, like one made with frosted glass and decorated with a plant motif.
A: Speaking of relaxing, how about the bathroom?
B: It shouldn't be too bright, so I would recommend indirect lighting. However, the bathroom needs to be bright enough for people to wash their body or shave, so the area around the mirror needs to be sufficiently illuminated.

A: ダイニングには、どんな照明を選びますか？
B: 部屋全体を明るくするためにはシンプルなシーリングライトが適切で、テーブルを照らすためのペンダントライトを組み合わせるとよいと思います。
A: 明かりの色はどんな色がいいですか？たとえば、昼光色と電球色とか？
B: 昼光色だと明るさは十分だけど、ちょっと冷たい感じがするから、電球色がいいです。キッチンなら、調理する素材の色と状態を確認できるように昼光色がいいと思います。
A: リビングはどうですか？

B: シャンデリアにフロアライトを足すことで、リラックスできるリビングのエレガントな雰囲気が高まるね。シャンデリアは、フロスト調ガラスを使って植物をモチーフにしたアールヌーボー風のデザインがいいです。
A: リラックスするという点では浴室はどうですか？
B: あまり明るくしないように間接照明がいいかも知れません。でも、身体をキレイにしたり、髭を剃ったりする場所でもあるので、鏡周りは明るい照明も欲しいですね。

Activities

Unit 10 Function

Activity 19   各種製品と機能 / Product Function

【解答例】

A: Do you have any ideas on how to make a dream vacuum cleaner?
B: How about if we could ride around on it?
A: That would be awesome. I think if it was self-driving and had a function to dispose of cockroaches while sucking up dust and garbage, that would be really helpful as well.
B: Great idea! You could get rid of cockroaches and stress at the same time. What problems would we need to overcome to add those functions?
A: Well, first you need to think about how to dispose of the cockroaches from the vacuum.
B: Yuck!
A: And we also have to think about how to capture them. It would be better not crush them.
B: Gross!
A: And while moving around on it, we have to be careful not to damage any of the surrounding furniture, so we need to add a sensor that can detect obstacles to prevent the machine from bumping into anything.
B: If it is going to be moving around, the cord might get in the way, so it probably should be battery operated.
A: It sounds like it might be better if it was an automated vacuum. Do we really need to ride on it?

A: 夢の掃除機について、何かアイデアはあるかな？
B: 乗って動き回れるとか？
A: それ、いいね。私は、ゴミを吸い取りながらゴキブリ退治もしてくれる自動運転掃除機があったらいいと思うなー。
B: いいアイデアだね！ゴキブリ退治と同時にストレスも解消できそうだね。じゃあ、その機能をつけるにあたっての問題点はなんだろう？
A: まず、どうやって捕ったゴキブリを捨てるか？だ。

B: うわ〜。
A: あと、ゴキブリの捕まえ方。できるだけつぶさないようにしたい。
B: げー。
A: 動き回る間に衝突して家具を傷つけないようにもしなくちゃいけないね。センサーで障害物を探知して家具にぶつからないようにする機能が必要だな。
B: 動くなら電源コードが邪魔だから、バッテリー式にしなくちゃね。
A: なんだか、自動運転の方がいいんじゃないかって気がしてきた。そもそも乗る必要あるのかな？

Activities

Unit 11　Application

Activity 20　コンペティションへの応募 / Application for a Competition

DREAM CG Art Award

テーマ：任意（CG で表現されたものに限る）

DREAM CG Art Award は、既存のアートや映像産業の枠を超えた「独創的」で「視覚的に美しい」CG 作品を募ります。

応募資格
- 2014 年以降に制作されたオリジナルの CG アート作品であること。
- 企業、個人、グループ、年齢、性別、職業、国籍等は問わない。
- 応募者は複数部門に応募可能。
- 第三者の作品（作品、映画、写真、音楽）を素材として使用する際は、権利者の許可を得ていることとする。
- 応募点数は 2 作品までとする。

募集期間：2015 年 5 月 20 日～ 8 月 20 日
入賞者特典：DREAM ギャラリーにて、10 日間作品が展示される。
応募費用：無料
応募方法：募集サイト上の「参加登録」ボタンから次へ進み、案内に従い応募手続きを行う。
用意するもの：作品キャプチャー画像：横幅 480 ～ 640pix 縦幅は指定なし。
※幅 640pix を越えるものは、自動圧縮。
ファイル形式：JPEG (RGB)、PNG、GIF
メールアドレス：問い合せ用に確実に連絡できるメールアドレス
プレゼンテーションシート：タイトル、コンセプト（200 ワード以内）、作者名もしくはグループ名、作者略歴（100 ワード以内）

※応募者は作品を応募した時点で所定の応募規定に同意したものとする。

【解答例】

プレゼンテーションシート

1. タイトル

   | Bugdroid |

2. コンセプト（200 ワード以内）

   > The author proposes "Bugdroid" made through gene manipulation of human beings and expresses their mode of living and appeals using 3D-CG. The author made details of joints to express the real movement of "Bugdroid", expressed in a beautiful but strange world. Still more, he emphasizes Bugdroid's hold on life by giving contrast to the organic material of the eyes and the cool-inorganic material of the surface.
   >
   > 人間に遺伝子操作を加えられた昆虫たち（Bugdroid）を想定して、その生態や魅力を 3DCG によって表現した。奇妙でありながらも美しいその世界観を表現するために、関節部などを細部まで造り込んで動きを感じさせ、瞳の有機的な質感と冷たく無機質な表面を対比させることによって Bugdroid の生命力を強調した。

3. 作者またはグループ名

   | Taro Kaitou |

Activities

4. 作者略歴（100 ワード以内）

Taro Kaitou is a graphic designer representing SAAC Incorporated. In 2000, he graduated from University of Art and Culture majoring in Graphic Design. Taro was awarded Grand Prize in the Fuji International Design Competition (in 2001), and in 2002 he won the Outstanding Performance Award at the TAKARA International Media Awards. Taro has been Art Director of the Mt. Fuji CG Art Project since 2013. His primary aim is to work combining human ingenuity and new technology to create bold new innovative designs.

皆藤太郎、株式会社 SAAC 代表、グラフィックデザイナー。2000 年、文化芸術大学を卒業。大学では、グラフィックデザインを専攻した。2001 年に富士国際グラフィックコンペ・グランプリ受賞、2002 年にタカラ国際メディアアワードにて優秀賞を受賞。2013 年から現在に至るまで、アートディレクターとして富士山 CG アートプロジェクトに参加している。人の感性と新しい技術を結びつける革新的なデザインを仕事の目標としている。